Framing and Presenting T

This fan by Linda Chilton is machine embroidered onto a dyed felt base which is stitched onto conservation mountboard. The fan is surrounded with a double conservation mount, the inner mount being only 3mm wide. A V-groove has been cut on the top mount and foam board fillets (which are covered with a tape manufactured from mountboard facing paper) are used both for effect and as a spacer. A further spacer has been used beneath the mounts to keep the object well away from the glass. Conservation glass has been used to prevent distortion of colour and to protect the textile from UV damage. A pale gold frame was chosen to reflect the colours within the embroidery.

Framing and Presenting Textile Art

By Annabelle Ruston

Published by the Fine Art Trade Guild
and A & C Black • London

First published in Great Britain in 2009
A & C Black Publishers Limited
38 Soho Square
London W1D 3HB
www.acblack.com

ISBN: 978-0-7136-8808-5

CIP Catalogue records for this book are available from the British Library and the US Library of Congress.

Researched and edited by Annabelle Ruston
Cover design by Sutchinda Rangsi Thompson
Page design by Tina Tong
Commissioning Editor: Susan James

Preface by Dr Susan Kay-Williams

Proof read and indexed by Sophie Page
Although every effort has been made to ensure that all the information in this publication is correct, the Fine Art Trade Guild and A&C Black cannot be held responsible for any errors or for financial transactions made on the basis of information in this publication.

Fine Art Trade Guild
16-18 Empress Place, London SW6 1TT
Tel: 020 7381 6616   Fax: 020 7381 2595
info@fineart.co.uk
www.fineart.co.uk

Printed and bound in China

contents

acknowledgements

This book would not have been possible without the support and expertise of Mal Reynolds GCF Adv, Harlequin Frames, a highly skilled textile framer and collector. Immeasurable thanks are due to Mal.

I would particularly like to thank the following: Lyn Hall GCF Adv, Fringe Arts, for researching and collating the glossary and working closely with me on the first draft; Mary Evans GCF, Applegarth Framing, for her invaluable comments; Elizabeth Karney, Freedom Framing, for her expertise on textile conservation; Rosie Sumner, Managing Director of the Fine Art Trade Guild, for making this book possible; and Louise Hay, Fine Art Trade Guild, for her help and support.

Sincere thanks are due to Ian Dixon GCF, Ian Dixon Bespoke Framing and Kai van Uffelen GCF CPF, van Uffelen Gallery and Picture Framing, for their comments on early drafts of this book. Barry Leveton GCF Adv has contributed hugely to this book; I am very thankful for his expert advice on conservation.

Vivian Kistler GCF was largely responsible for the first draft of the glossary.

Most of the illustrations are photographs of artwork in the private collections of Mal Reynolds GCF Adv and Lyn Hall GCF Adv. I am very grateful to both of them for putting up with the disruption that the photography entailed.

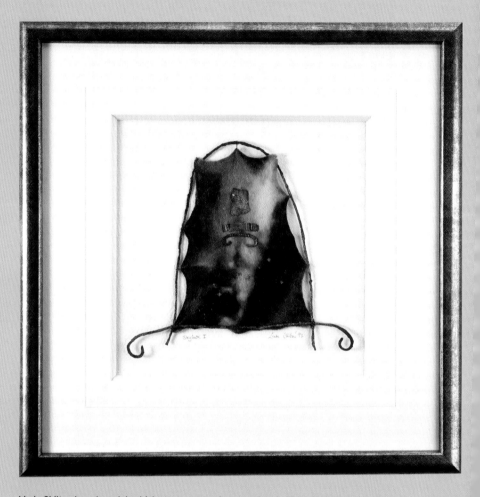

Linda Chilton has shaped dyed felt over a copper frame and embellished it with silver and other metals. The artwork has been stitched onto conservation mountboard with fishing line at points where it lay flat against the board. A V-groove has been carved onto the mount and foam board fillets are covered with tape manufactured from mountboard facing paper, to ensure that the colour and texture match perfectly. Conservation glass was used and the copper frame reflects the metals within the artwork.

preface

Textiles have a very important role to play in our social history – from court to commoner, they give us a fascinating insight into so much more than just a stitching lexicon: the plants that have been identified in the Hunting of the Unicorn tapestries; the changing sources of red dye: madder from the east, cochineal from the west, both reflecting the history of exploration; the journey of silk from China to the rest of the world; and the importance of the wool trade in Britain and western Europe. Then there is the range of textiles: church vestments and courtly robes to designer gowns, commissioned objects such as tapestries and furniture and, on the smaller scale, from simple educational samplers to exquisitely worked pieces of hand embroidered whitework or goldwork.

Every textile artist, amateur or professional, knows that, for them, much of the pleasure in a piece of textile art is in the creation of the work itself. Whether it is the most straightforward counted cross stitch, or a stunning 3D multi-media commission, its creation will have involved many hours of work. For the amateur textile artist the process can even be a form of therapy, enabling those for whom it is not their day job to become relaxed through the total immersion in this most absorbing of activities.

Such enthusiasts will not count the hours they take to produce a finished piece, and certainly not translate that into a cost, a fact which has an interesting repercussion when people are ready to display their work. Forgetting about what it has 'cost' them to make something can mean that, when it comes to framing, it can be all too easy simply to rush out and buy a cheap frame without consideration for the requirements of the textile.

Unfortunately, most 'instant' frames are really only made for flat prints or photographs that adhere to standard dimensions. They do not allow a three dimensional piece to lie clear of the glass, the mountboard is only of standard quality and so on. As a result, there is a high chance that people will spoil the presentation of their textiles (and possibly their longevity) because they have not recognised the necessary investment in good display.

But the second reason for this 'instant' approach may be because, for most people, their local picture framer may not be a Guild Commended Framer who holds the Advanced Accreditation in Textile Framing, so they are scared of taking a textile to them, for fear of what will be done to their precious artwork. Horror stories of perceived poor service always seem more prevalent than those of satisfied customers.

So, as the textile arts begin to see a resurgence, this book comes as a timely addition.

This is a very practical book to aid framers, and hopefully encourage more Guild Commended Framers to take the additional Advanced Accreditation in Textile Framing, and then make themselves known to textile artists in their area. The example projects at the end of the book show some innovative solutions to displaying a wide variety of textiles which should serve to encourage those who are willing to learn and experiment.

But I believe the book also has value for textile artists and small collectors. It can really help to spread the word about why it is important to mount and display textiles appropriately.

It can also teach people how to prevent or at least reduce the likelihood of the 'nasties', such as damp, dirt, decay and insects, that could be waiting to attack inappropriately displayed pieces. This is important because, while not everyone needs or wants to display their personal work or collected items to museum standard, few of us want to see pieces disintegrating before our eyes. And, unfortunately, textiles do not have to be hundreds of years old before they show signs of dirt and degradation.

Learning about why textiles should not rest against glass, or why glue should be used sparingly, if at all, is as useful to textile enthusiasts as it is to framers. We want to enjoy textiles adorning our walls, not just wrapped in acid-free tissue and shut away in dark rooms, where they may last longer but cannot be enjoyed. To achieve this we need the support of a trained and empathetic framer, who will listen to the needs of the customer to find an appropriate solution.

At the Royal School of Needlework we always have work, from the collection and by recent apprentices, on display. This inspires our working environment and is a fabulous insight into the history of embroidery and into the accomplishment of our apprentices and our studio through its 135 year history. It is wonderful to see what can be created with 'just' a needle and thread. By being displayed, the pieces are also available for visitors and students to see and study. We believe that it is vital to have access to good examples on display when learning a new technique, because this offers so much more than just seeing pictures in a book. Sometimes pieces come to us in their original frame and this can add to our appreciation of the work as well as help with telling their story.

With the help of this book, I hope that many more framers and textile lovers will jointly be involved in developing new, innovative and appropriate ways of framing and displaying both contemporary and historical textile art so they will continue to have a story to tell well into the future.

Dr Susan Kay-Williams
Chief Executive
Royal School of Needlework

"Eternal Grace" stitched by
Jean Julier of the Japanese
Embroiderers' Guild
(©Japanese Embroidery
Center).

Japanese embroidery is worked on silk with silk threads and demands great care when handling. The work is stitched whilst under great tension on a sewing frame, so, when framing, it is important to tension the fabric to ensure that the stitches stay tight and square. This piece of work was padded over conservation quality foam board and then laced. Black suedette board was chosen because of its density of colour and similarity to the wig of the geisha. Creative corners were cut to enhance the embroidery and reflect the shape of the gown, and small pieces of hand-coloured board were inlaid into the corners to pull the whole presentation together. A double mount was used to ensure that the padded fabric did not touch the glass. Conservation glass was used to protect the image and finally, a black bamboo frame was used to continue the oriental theme.

"Rising Peony" stitched by Jean Julier of the Japanese Embroiderers' Guild
(©Midori Matsushima).

The embroidery was stretched, padded and laced over conservation foam board to return it to its original tension. The design of the mount was taken from the piece itself. Conservation board was used for a double mount with a spacer in between to ensure that the fabric did not touch the glass. The top mount was cut with a series of small openings running around the aperture and a piece of board was placed beneath these holes, which was painted in varying tones from the embroidery. A partial V-groove was used to anchor these openings around the image. Conservation glass protects the image and a traditional silver frame with mauve overtones finishes off the theme.

introduction

This book is aimed both at professional framers wanting to develop their ability to frame textile art and at textile artists wishing to know more about presenting and protecting their work. It is not, however, a basic picture framing manual and does not describe, for example, how to cut and join the four sides of a frame, or how to cut windowmounts. Appendix 4: Useful further reading suggests some titles that will help teach basic framing skills, and Appendix 5: Framing training, lists courses accredited by the Fine Art Trade Guild.

Framing is a vast and fascinating topic. Many volumes have been written about it and framers whose careers have spanned half a century are still learning new ideas. The only aspects of framing which are discussed in this book are those that are unique to the framing of fabric art.

This book describes techniques for supporting and displaying fabric art and indicates when each might be appropriate. Problematic areas are discussed, as are the materials and equipment required to carry out each technique. New types of textiles and fabric art are being developed all the time and it is important to be aware of the different methods required to handle this vast range. The glossary gives an indication of the diversity that you may come across.

The Fine Art Trade Guild's Five Levels of Framing are referred to throughout this book. These standards are a benchmark of good practice that help framers explain their choices to customers, and reassure customers that their artwork is being looked after properly. They are also useful in the event of litigation, as they help explain when particular materials and techniques are appropriate. The levels are laid out in full in Appendix 1: Five Levels of Framing; it is important that anyone undertaking framing work has a good understanding of these.

As I hope this book conveys, the limit is your imagination when choosing materials, techniques and designs that will display fabric art in its full glory. One of the joys of this type of work is that there are few hard and fast rules, apart from the one golden, immutable one that must guide all your choices: the framer's role is to protect and display artwork, not to alter its original condition.

Annabelle Ruston
Fine Art Trade Guild

"Butterfly Panel" stitched by Jean Julier of the Japanese Embroiderers' Guild
(©Japanese Embroidery Center).

This panel is all about the vibrancy and richness of gold work in combination with small amounts of colour. Working with black fabrics is problematic because of their tendency to pick up dust and it is very difficult to match blacks within the frame. Black board with a shiny finish was used because it complemented the black fabric. The mount is narrow at the sides and deeper top and bottom to accentuate the panel-shape of the artwork. A bamboo frame continues the theme.

chapter one
before framing

There are various points to consider before choosing a frame, to ensure that the fabric art is displayed to its best advantage and protected against deterioration. Very careful scrutiny is required at this stage.

Note should be taken of any imperfections and consideration given as to how these might be rectified, or their effects minimised. Some framers take photographs of imperfections before they start, so there is no chance of customers blaming them for these later on. At the very least, blemishes should be noted on a job ticket which is signed by both framer and customer. Blemishes tend to be magnified by glass, so are more noticeable when framed.

Framers are not responsible for repairing faults. The framer's role is to protect and display artwork, not to alter its original condition. The person who owns the fabric art should handle any cleaning, trimming, cutting threads, filling in stitches, etc. The risks to fabric from intervention are too great, and framers could risk their reputation and solvency by interfering. However, framers should be able to advise customers about any action that is required.

Fabric art should be handled and stored carefully. Natural oils and perspiration in our hands can cause stains to appear over time, so gloves should be worn when handling valuable work. Hands must be clean and rings and other jewellery must not be of a style that may snag fabrics.

It is advisable to place work on a piece of white card while inspecting it, as this shows up colours as well as any dirty marks. Begin by checking the front and then turn the fabric over and carefully examine the back. Holding it up to the light may also make problems apparent.

Dirt, discolouration and cleaning
Fabric art can be transformed by cleaning. It can help preserve fabric by removing harmful acids, and can re-invigorate the pile and shape of the stitches. Even fabric that does not look dirty can look a lot better once cleaned.

Washing should always be carried out by the owner of the fabric art, not the framer, while surface cleaning can be done by a framer. If a framer feels that a piece would benefit from washing, the customer should be told and advice given.

a) Surface cleaning
Wool may be dry cleaned, though good results can be achieved by just going over it with a hand-held vacuum cleaner on a low setting. It is advisable to cover the work with a meshed plastic grid (available from craft shops), or a

"Wisteria and Chrysanthemum Fan" stitched by Jean Julier of the Japanese Embroiderers' Guild (©Japanese Embroidery Center).

This Japanese embroidery is stitched on 'cloth of silver', a fabric which incorporates silk threads, paper and silver. It is very rigid and highly expensive, so great care must be taken whilst handling it. A simple double mount distances the fabric from the glass and a frame incorporating both silver and gold enhances the presentation.

net, that will hold the stitches in place while you vacuum. (It is possible to make your own grid by stretching wide-meshed canvas over a strainer.)

Little suction cleaners and bellows used for cleaning cameras and keyboards can be handy, gentle tools for removing surface dirt. Soft mops and make-up brushes can also be used. If you work over a clean white towel you may be surprised by how much dirt is removed by gentle brushing and blowing.

b) Washing

Before washing, you need to be sure that this is appropriate for the fabric and threads in question. Otherwise, fabrics may shrink and colours may run. Testing for colourfastness is discussed in the section on 'Colourfastness', in Chapter 3: Squaring needlepoint, p46. Some experienced picture framers and stitchers feel that the only sewn fabric art that can safely be washed is modern aida cloth sewn with modern embroidery threads. It is just too risky to attempt washing any other materials.

Work that has been produced by hand may be discoloured by grease from the stitcher's hands and perspiring fingers, and there may be a mark left by an embroidery hoop or frame (see section on 'Embroidery hoops', p23).

Marks will be particularly prominent on fine fabrics with unworked backgrounds, or pale materials. Even if finger marks are not visible on hand-sewn works, oils from hands will have permeated the materials, so, if practicable, it is advisable to clean stitched fabrics before framing, otherwise stains may develop later on.

Cotton should be hand-washed using lukewarm distilled or de-ionised water and mild soap suds with no detergent (tap water may leave a brown tide mark when dry). It is possible to check that all the soap is rinsed away by testing with a pH paper strip, of the type used to test chlorine levels in swimming pools. Lay the strip on the damp fabric and keep rinsing until the strip reads neutral.

Never use fabric conditioner or starch when washing fabric art. These products can introduce chemicals into the frame that may have harmful longterm effects, and starch can encourage insect infestation and mould as these feed off the starch.

c) Stains and stain removers

It is inadvisable to use stain removers on fabric art as these products may fade the fabric. Stains should be removed by professional textile conservators, with specialist equipment such as vacuum probes, tanks in which fabric can remain under constant supervision during cleaning, special fabric cleaning tables and so on. Try to identify the cause of any stains, as this may indicate how best to remove the marks.

"Kusadama" stitched by Jean Julier of the Japanese Embroiderers' Guild (©Japanese Embroidery Center).

The artwork was padded and laced over conservation foam board and a simple double mount is the backdrop for the vibrancy of the stitching. The gold frame with a ribbed sight edge reflects the colours of the gold threads.

d) Weakened textiles
Textiles that have become brittle and discoloured have probably been kept in unfavourable conditions causing the fibres to break down. This process cannot be reversed and it is important not to put further strain on fragile fabrics when stretching them, as they may tear, so they should be sewn onto a pre-stretched donor cloth (see the section on 'Fragile and valuable fabrics', p70). Museum or Conservation Level framing will not reverse the process of deterioration, but will help protect the artwork. Washing may help to preserve the fabric by balancing its pH levels, but cleaning old or damaged textiles should always be undertaken by a textile conservator.

Pressing
Pressing can improve the appearance of many types of fabric art, but unless you proceed with caution great damage can be done.
Here are some guidelines:

1) Fabrics should be pressed at different temperatures as the surface texture and colours of some fabrics can be affected by heat. For example, dyed linen can become dark and flat-looking if pressed at too hot a temperature and wool scorches easily.
2) Fabrics should be pressed face-down and laid between two soft clean cloths. Never iron the front of any fabric art.
3) Pressing should be carried out with a gentle 'padding' action to avoid disturbing or damaging the stitches. Some people prefer to iron fabric on the diagonal, as the point of the iron can catch the threads, while others feel that this can stretch the material out of shape and prevent it from laying flat.
4) The ironing process is accelerated by ironing through a damp cloth, though you must be sure that the colours will not run. Testing for colourfastness is discussed in the section on 'Colourfastness', in Chapter 3: Squaring needlepoint, p46. Proceed by pressing lightly with a moderately hot iron; then remove the damp cloth and allow the fabric to dry properly before framing.
5) If needle art has been flattened during the working process and pressing will not correct the condition, test for colourfastness, then try mounting it onto a frame and applying steam from behind, or place a wet cloth over an upright hot iron and hold the fabric over this. The steam passes through the work from the wrong to the right side and lifts the threads. Steaming can also be used to lift flattened velvet fibres.
6) A spiked velvet board is essential for ironing velvet.

Mould and insects

There is no point in framing textiles that are mouldy or home to insects, as they will continue to deteriorate, both aesthetically and physically. Check for infestation before you start. Old fabrics, those of unknown origin and any that have been stored in damp or dirty conditions are the most likely to be affected.

If you suspect that a fabric is infested, isolate it immediately. Examine it outside and look carefully for signs of infestation and the smell of damp and decay. Then seal it in a heavy-duty polythene bag, removing as much air as possible.

If you own the infested textile you might consider freezing it overnight (framers should not do this without the customer's permission). Bring the item back to room temperature the next day without handling. Current research seems to indicate that no damage occurs to the cellular structure of textile fibres during freezing. Freezing can halt both mite and moth damage.

Mould not only looks unsightly, but also causes deterioration. It can sometimes be killed by exposure to heat, but this won't work once the mould has worked its way right into the fibres. Bear in mind that heat can cause fabrics to fade or shrink and will seal in stains: if in doubt do not treat the mould but pass the item to a professional textile conservator.

The safest ways of killing active mould spores are:

- leave affected items exposed to light in dry conditions
- hold a hair dryer at a distance and dry out the mould until it is reduced to dust
- thorough surface cleaning using a low-powered vacuum cleaner and protective mesh.

Textile conservators do not generally use chemicals to kill mould and insects, partly because of their potentially damaging effects on both fabric and the people using them, and partly because insects are becoming immune to fumigation chemicals. Conservators use the methods mentioned above, sometimes in conjunction with wet or dry cleaning and freezing.

Wool is prone to moth infestation, though most modern wool has been treated against this, and wool is unlikely to attract mould. Cotton is safe from moth infestation but is vulnerable to silverfish and mould. Carpet beetles, of which there are several varieties, can infest textiles, and woodworm living in wooden frames and back boards can cause damage to the textiles within.

In the past, needlepoint canvases were stiffened with sugar solution (today, size is used instead). Sugar attracts insects, so old needlepoint that shows signs of insect infestation should be passed to a textile conservator for cleaning. While eating the sugar, insects also consume fabric fibres, causing them to weaken (which is another reason why old needlepoint should be handled with care).

If fabric art is framed to Museum or Conservation Level, the framing package is sealed, and, if the artwork is hung in normal conditions (see glossary for definition), the chances of infestation by mould or insects are minimised.

Missing and travelling stitches

Holding the work up to the light should help reveal both missing and travelling stitches.

Search carefully for missing stitches and the stitcher should fill these in where possible, as once the fabric is properly squared and framed they are likely to become more prominent. Missing stitches can jump out at you from under glazing, due to a magnifying effect.

Travelling stitches are where the stitcher has not cut off the thread each time, but has, in effect, made a giant stitch at the back of the work in order to sew another part of it. Once the work is laid down on a base, these threads will show more clearly. Travelling stitches can also prevent the correct tension being attained when the item is stretched.

Either the stitcher should carefully cut and sew these in, or, if the work is of no commercial or sentimental value, they could be cut and glued back with PVA adhesive. Threads must be stitched at Commended Level and above, but it is acceptable to use adhesive at Budget and Minimum Levels.

You can minimise the effect of travelling stitches by choosing an undermount in a shade that will help disguise them, but bear in mind that a dark

before framing

This embroidery by Lorna J Bateman has a double mount. The overall mount size was 15mm bigger than required because when the mounts were cut, the 15mm edge was scored and raised so that a box effect was achieved. The small squares in the corners were removed and the box was taped up with gummed paper tape. This means that the rebate is from the same board as the mounts which looks very neat.

undermount may alter the colours in the whole piece. Padding can sometimes help hide travelling stitches (see the section on 'Padding', p62).

Loose threads and fragments

Long loose threads may show at the front. The stitcher should cut these away if they are superfluous, or, using a needle, carefully push them under an area of colour that will hide them.

Check whether there are any fragments of thread poking through to the front of the fabric, which have been accidentally carried through by the needle. These will show and look unattractive if they are light on dark or dark on light; they occur because one shade is sewn first and fragments are picked up when a second colour is sewn over this. Thread fragments can be removed with tweezers.

Knots

Knots at the back of needle art can mean that the fabric will not lie flat. A layer of polyester padding at the back can disguise knots, or you can cut small indents into a mountboard support in which the knots will sit. This can

In this piece of stump work by Lorna J Bateman, wires and padding are used as a base for ribbons and threads up to 30mm deep. The work is surrounded by a simple single mount incorporating a V-groove. Foam board fillets lead your eye into the picture, and a large spacer beneath the mount provides depth. The silver frame with a deep rebate has a slightly distressed finish revealing a red base colour.

weaken the mountboard so is only recommended if the fabric is very bulky and the customer is against padding.

Needle art which is very uneven at the back can be stretched over stretcher bars, which means that the knots will not be pressed against a support, so they should be less prominent.

Taped edges

Some stitchers edge fabrics with tape to prevent fraying and unravelling during sewing. Acid-laden self-adhesive tape such as masking tape is often used, so this should be removed. It should not be necessary to replace the tape as fraying will not occur once the item is framed.

Framers should remove tape while the customer is still present, to see what lies beneath. Once the tape has gone an acidic adhesive residue may remain, which should ideally be washed by the owner of the textile. Washing should remove the stickiness, though some staining will probably remain.

Stitchers should be advised to use hand-sewn borders of binding ribbon for future projects, but if this is too time-consuming then at least gummed-paper tape with a water-soluble adhesive should be used.

Imperfections and holes

Silks and fine cottons are prone to imperfections in the weave and discolouration in the woven twine. Search for these blemishes and make a note of them before framing, so that you can be sure when they occurred.

Holes will show when fabrics are held up to the light. These can sometimes be disguised by the right colour of undermount. Stretching fabrics is likely to put pressure on holes and make them worse, so consider what caused the hole. If the fabric is vulnerable you may decide to attach it to a pre-stretched donor fabric.

Embroidery hoops

Embroidery hoops can sometimes break fibres; in cases where this problem is severe you might choose to attach the artwork to a donor fabric.

Framers should try to encourage regular customers to adhere to good practice with embroidery hoops.

It is a good idea to remove the hoop after each sewing session and to replace it in a slightly different position each time, as this helps minimise hoop marks.

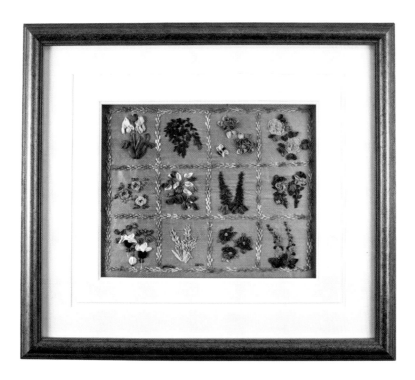

This sampler by Lorna J Bateman was worked on silk with a variety of techniques and materials. The silk base was extended with donor cloths so that it was big enough to lace over board and padding was placed behind to even out any tension anomalies. A neutral 'channel mount' was chosen because the shadows of the channels give definition and detail. A foam board spacer was inserted under the mount.

Because the design of this patchwork is evocative of the Art Deco era, the mount was chosen to reflect this. Dark blue and gold lower mounts mirror the fabric, while a neutral double mount provides visual space. Small pieces of mountboard arranged in the corners continue the Art Deco theme.

It is important to use an embroidery hoop that is sufficiently large; stitchers should use the largest hoop that the fabric will accommodate. There is a tendency to use inexpensive small hoops that come right up to the edge of the design, meaning that either any marks will be visible once the item is framed, some sewn edges will be lost in an effort to hide the marks or you may have to risk washing the item. The cost of larger hoops is minimal compared with the time and effort required to create a piece of needle art.

The correct way round

In the case of some dyed fabrics and batiks it is hard to tell which side is the front. Make sure that you know which way you want the fabric to face before framing. Signatures can help indicate which is the front.

Trimming

Think twice before trimming the edges off fabric art so that it fits into a frame. This irretrievably alters the original condition of the artwork, so can affect its value in the long term. Even if you have stitched the work yourself it is better not to trim it, as this limits the ways in which the piece can be displayed in the future.

Framers must never trim customers' work without their prior agreement in writing and should ardently discourage customers from trimming work they

own. If a customer insists on trimming a textile, it is best for the framer to hand the customer the scissors and for them to do it.

Protective sprays

You can buy protective sprays that the manufacturers recommend as a method of protecting fabrics from decay. However, textile conservators strongly advise against spraying fabric art as the chemical make-up of these sprays is complex and their longterm effects are unknown. Sprays interfere with the original condition of the fabric, which is not good practice. Careful cleaning and framing to Museum or Conservation Level are much safer ways of protecting artwork.

Painted fabrics

Painted fabrics need stretching, but not squaring. When stretching painted fabric you must be gentle so that the paint does not crack when pulled.

The paint may crack if it is exposed to the heat of an iron, even through a cloth, so it is advisable not to press painted textiles.

Previous framing

One of the worst enemies of textiles is inadequate framing materials and techniques. Acid-laden adhesive, wood and board, as well as over-tensioning, can do untold damage, so textiles should be removed from inadequate frames as quickly as possible.

Luckily, adhesive can lose its hold over the years, so this task may be quite straightforward. Adhesives made prior to about 1920 tend to be animal or vegetable in origin, rather than chemical, which means that they will be water soluble. Be careful not to put any pressure on fabric when removing it; if you can't remove tape or board easily, the item should be passed on to a conservator.

In the past textiles were often mounted onto stretcher bars with metal tacks. If the wood has become damp it may have stained the fabric, and tacks can leave rust marks and broken fibres. Be careful not to damage textiles when removing tacks; these may have become thoroughly embedded over time, so you may have to exert strong pressure. (A tack remover is a handy tool; it should be held lengthwise to the stretcher bars with a piece of mount-board underneath to protect the textile.)

Washing removes some staining and restores the pH balance of fabrics. This should be carried out by the owner of the textile, not the framer, and it should be reiterated that washing is not suitable for all textiles. If in doubt, hand the item over to a professional conservator for washing.

While not all evidence of damage can be removed, re-framing textiles to Museum or Conservation Level will help protect them against future deterioration. For example, if an old textile is taken off its stretcher bars and sewn onto a pre-stretched donor fabric, no more pressure will be exerted onto the broken threads and rusty holes made by the tacks. The damage will not be eradicated, but it should be hidden by the new frame, and further deterioration should be halted.

chapter two
framing

Framing has two roles: to aesthetically enhance artwork and to help preserve it. Even the most beautiful and painstakingly sewn fabric art can be demeaned by a cramped and badly designed frame, whereas the right frame can make a piece of humble cross stitch look like a work of art.

Low grade framing materials and inappropriate techniques can cause untold damage to artwork. For example, masking tape and other low-quality self-adhesive tapes can leave a residue that will discolour artwork and cause it to deteriorate. Artwork that is stuck onto poor-quality board will also deteriorate as a result of exposure to dangerous acids. Fabric art that is badly stretched may weaken and tear, and moisture that is transmitted to artwork from glass that is too close can cause mould and decay to set in.

The best way of ensuring that your artwork will look good and be protected with the appropriate frame is to choose a professional framer. Framers who have qualified as Guild Commended Framers (GCFs) have passed a rigorous exam, so your artwork should be safe in their hands. The Fine Art Trade Guild will recommend a qualified GCF framer near you.

Conservation framing materials and techniques help preserve artwork and offer protection from potentially damaging atmospheric pollutants. Artwork of commercial or sentimental value deserves to be framed to Conservation Level (see Appendix 1: Five Levels of Framing).

A few extremely experienced framers have passed an advanced GCF module in Textile Framing, which means that they should be able to handle even the most challenging fabric framing work. See Appendix 2: Advanced Accreditation, Textile Framing to find out what this qualification entails.

Below are some points to consider when choosing a framer and a frame.

Which of the Five Levels of Framing?
Of course, not all fabric art is intended to last for generations. Sometimes a basic framing job is all that is required. However, all frames should be structurally sound and blemish-free; this is the least that customers should expect. A frame in which, for example, the artwork comes unattached and slips down into one corner, is of no use to anyone. This is where the Fine Art Trade Guild's Five Levels of Framing come in.

The point of these important standards is to help customers choose the right type of frame for their artwork, and to help framers explain why they are recommending particular materials and techniques. The levels are explained in full in Appendix 1: Five Levels of Framing.

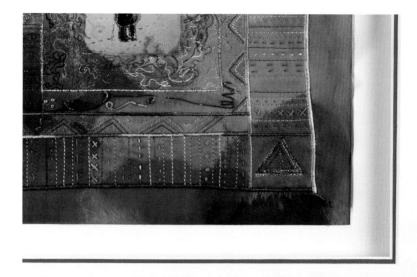

This textile was made by Karen Hall with layers of silk chiffon machine embroidered onto dyed felt. A triple mount is used, the central one being made up of four different coloured boards inlaid together to reflect the colour changes in the picture. There is a deep spacer between the second and third mounts to accommodate the central figures.

Because amateurs produce much fabric art, there is a tendency to regard a lot of it as non-valuable. To correct this view it is only necessary to see old samplers, produced under duress by our young ancestors, fetching large sums at auction. In any case, most fabric art is unique. Fabric art is easy to damage and premature deterioration can easily set in. Before choosing which level artwork should be framed to, bear in mind that today's disposables are often tomorrow's collectibles.

Fabric art is prone to damage by: UV light, heat, humidity, insects and poor-quality framing. Textiles can be protected by conservation materials and techniques; each of the Five Levels of Framing offers differing levels of protection.

If customers specifically request framing to a lower level than the framer recommends, the disadvantages of such work should be discussed. It should be remembered that inadequate jobs can be a false economy as the work may need further attention in years to come.

Some framers, mindful of their carefully developed reputations, will refuse to carry out work to a lower level than their recommendation. Others will do the work, but put disclaimers on the back of frames to prevent future litigation.

Image size

You must decide the exact image size to be visible. There are no inflexible rules surrounding this decision; it depends upon factors such as the boldness of the subject, the texture of the stitches, the size of the work, the moulding

to be used, where the work is to hang and, above all, personal taste. Work can be flattered by a wide expanse of plain fabric surrounding it and the effect can be stylish and dramatic.

Some framers apply this standard rule: measure the stitched or printed area and then allow a border of between 25mm and 35mm on all four sides. However, this is only a guideline.

Do not forget that about 5mm will be hidden by the lip of the moulding or the bevelled edge of the windowmount. Many stitchers do forget this and are disappointed to find that their framed work is slightly smaller than they had anticipated.

Windowmounts and alternative methods of spacing

Windowmounts have two main functions, one aesthetic and the other structural:

1) They provide visual space around artwork that allows the design to 'breathe'. Windowmounts can emphasise particular colours and can be cut to echo shapes in the artwork. Mountboard comes in many textures and can be covered with fabric.
2) Mounts distance artwork from glazing, which is important as moisture may form on the inside of the glazing as the temperature and humidity change, which can damage artwork.

Mountboard comes in three main qualities, which are identified in the Fine Art Trade Guild's Mountboard Standards. These are, in descending order of quality: cotton museum; conservation; and standard. The main features of each are outlined in the glossary to this book and they can be seen in full at *www.fineart.co.uk/mountboardstandards.aspx*. There are many boards available that do not meet even the Guild's minimum standard for mountboard and these should never be used in framing. Inferior boards are laden with acids that cause irreparable damage to artwork; they will eventually migrate onto the fabric, causing its fibres to discolour and weaken.

Standard rectangular windowmounts are generally twice as wide as the border of plain fabric surrounding the image, though this is a matter of personal taste and is a guideline, not a rule.

Below are some options to consider when choosing windowmounts, or alternative methods of spacing:

This antique silk screen was made around 1920 and is owned by Anne Milton MP. The artwork was stitched onto cotton then laced over a padded piece of MDF. A 25mm wood fillet is fitted inside the frame to provide depth.

1) Oval, circular and irregular apertures

If you anticipate difficulties in squaring the item or lining up the weave it can be a good idea to opt for an oval or circular aperture, as this will not show up the unevenness as much as straight-cut edges would. Oval and circular windows can also be used to hide stubborn marks, such as those left by embroidery hoops.

Interestingly cut mounts, with steps and niches, can be used to conceal imperfections. If cut to mirror aspects of the design, these can look very effective.

2) Double and multiple mounts

Double and multiple mounts can flatter artwork, as well as ensure that fabrics with 3D embellishments do not touch the glazing. The lower mounts, which only project a few millimetres, give you the opportunity to reflect colours in the artwork.

3) Textured and covered mounts

Some people feel that cardboard windowmounts do not flatter textile art. Mounts can be covered with textiles or bookcloth, and mountboard manufacturers provide a range of suedette- and velvet-covered boards. See the section entitled 'Fabric-covered mounts' later in this chapter for a brief description of how to make this type of mount.

4) Spacers and fillets

'Spacers' create depth, which helps distance artwork from glazing and they can look aesthetically pleasing. Spacers can be used in combination with a windowmount, and be placed either underneath it or on top of it, but under the lip of the moulding. They can also be used instead of a windowmount. Spacers are normally made from mountboard or foam board, and lengths of acrylic spacer can be bought from framing wholesalers.

Needlepoints sewn with thick woollen stitches are not traditionally surrounded by windowmounts. It is generally agreed that spacers are aesthetically preferable for this type of work.

Samplers and other designs which are stitched with elaborate borders do not require windowmounts aesthetically. However, the artwork still needs to be distanced from the glazing, so spacers should be used instead.

Fillets or slips, often gold in colour, are positioned around the inner edges of windowmounts and are an attractive way of distancing work from glazing. Fillets are, in effect, thin wooden mouldings.

5) When to use unbuffered mountboard

The section on 'Mountboard' under 'Types of support', Chapter 4: Stretching fabric art, p53 explains why unbuffered mountboard should be used when framing protein-based fabrics to Museum Level. This type of board should be used for the windowmount, support and undermount.

Fabric-covered mounts

The limit is your imagination when selecting fabrics to cover windowmounts, though this must obviously enhance the qualities of the artwork, rather than overpower it. Raw silk, for example, creates an opulent look that flatters Oriental paintings on silk, while muted linens can look good around old samplers.

It can be effective to mirror one of the stitched colours, rather than the backing fabric, when covering a windowmount.

If you don't mind an uncovered bevel, you can dry mount fabric onto mount-board before cutting the aperture. This can look fine if the mountboard and the fabric are close in colour, or if a contrast is required. There must be a brand-new blade in the mountcutter so that the fabric will not fray.

Below are two methods for covering windowmounts, including the edges of the aperture:

1) Covering bevelled windowmounts using a vacuum press

Cut your mount with a bevelled aperture and keep the centre fall-out. Brush wet glue over the mount and bevel; then, when the glue is almost dry, position the fabric over the mount and carefully press the centre fall-out back in.

Put the mount into your press for a couple of minutes and you will find that the centre fall-out has pushed the fabric neatly against the bevel.

Cut the fabric away from the aperture, leaving a border of 10 to 15mm. Use a sharp knife to mitre the corners of the fabric; then fold it neatly back and glue it into position.

2) Covering bevelled windowmounts, including ovals

Cut a piece of fabric a few centimetres larger than the windowmount and pin it in place around the outside edges, sticking pins lightly into the core of the mountboard. Take care that the grain of the fabric is straight in both directions.

Turn the mount over and run a bead of adhesive around the outside edge; then pull the fabric onto this and allow it to dry before removing the pins. Then cut into the fabric at the centre of the aperture, and continue cutting it away, leaving a border of about 10mm around all the edges.

If you are creating a mount with an oval aperture, cut little 'teeth' into the border, a few millimetres apart. Run a bead of adhesive around the back of the aperture and pull the teeth through and onto this. Otherwise, just mitre the corners and carefully fold the fabric back and glue it in place.

Strips of board under the windowmount

In many cases there is not sufficient spare fabric to stretch the artwork to the same size as the outer measurement of the windowmount. If the stretched textile is smaller than the windowmount, the latter may not lie flat, but will

This slightly whacky textile by Peggy Crowley is made from fabric, leather, plastic, lace, felt and machine embroidery. It was stitched onto conservation mountboard with a variety of coloured threads to suit the different areas of stitching. A wide single mount incorporating a V-groove and foam board fillets gives a simple contemporary feel to the work. A spacer beneath the mount creates distance and a moulding with a deep rebate was chosen.

slope down into the frame. In these cases, spacers should be concealed under the windowmount, so that it can lie flat.

Spacers are generally made from strips of foam board or mountboard, to the same thickness as the stretched fabric. These are normally stuck to the undermount with double-sided tape. The strips of board will hold the stretched fabric in place, ensuring that it stays straight and doesn't slip down in the frame.

Undermounts and box linings

In many cases the undermount and support will be hidden by the needlework being framed. However, when framing 3D items and clothing, which require a box-frame, the undermount will be visible, and the sides of the box will probably also show (depending upon the frame design). Undermounts are also visible when artwork is float-mounted.

Just as many framers do not feel that paper-covered windowmounts flatter fabric art, many do not like paper-covered undermounts and box linings for fabrics. Suedette mountboard is a popular option, as this handles easily and

Pieces of this mixed-media embroidery were glued onto mountboard with EVA glue. A mount was then cut to accommodate the 12 squares and fit into the ready-made frame which was chosen because of its ethnic appearance and colouring.

is supplied ready-made, so there is no need to cover the mountboard. However, customers on a budget tend to insist on a plain mountboard box lining.

Framers who handle a lot of fabric art tend to hold a wide range of velvets and linens which they use to line box-frames. Velvet looks sumptuous, while the tones and texture of linen can flatter old samplers, which were often sewn onto linen-type fabrics. Suedette is a versatile material, but it can have an open weave which means that glue can easily soak through. Framers who use suedette advise sourcing a heavy-duty version from wall-hanging specialists.

Just as when covering windowmounts with fabric, you must be careful that the grain is running at right angles. Some framers stick fabric over under-mounts with PVA, while others find it quicker to use self-adhesive mount-board or spray-on adhesive.

In the section on 'Presentation' in Chapter 4: Stretching fabric art, p61, there is a discussion of the effects of coloured mountboard and padding under stretched fabric art. This section focuses on cases where the undermount will be hidden by the artwork. Later in the same chapter there is a discussion on how to stretch fragile and valuable fabrics, which includes information on the appropriate 'donor' fabrics.

The section on 'Mountboard' under 'Types of support', Chapter 4: Stretching fabric art, p63 explains why unbuffered mountboard should be used when framing protein-based fabrics to Musuem Level. This type of board should be used for the support and undermount, as well as for the windowmount.

Mouldings and build-ups

The rebate of the moulding will often come into direct contact with fabric art (this is not the case with works on paper as paper is never folded over onto the back of the undermount). The acid in wood can stain fabric so it is advisable to line the moulding with protective foil-backed sealing tape or strips of mountboard. Some framers coat the rebate with a few layers of commercial sealant, though spirit-based sealant may be acidic so not suitable for conservation work. Acrylic or gesso paint are better solutions.

Once fabric art has been stretched over a support it can be too thick to be held by the rebate of many standard mouldings. However, it is possible to build-up mouldings with a width of 25mm or more (thinner mouldings would not be strong enough to support the build-up).

Some framers stock lengths of timber ranging up to 20mm especially for making build-ups, while others prefer to make boxes out of foam board. Wooden build-ups should be cut to the length of each piece of moulding and attached before the frame is assembled using wood glue and pins. The build-up should then be stained, sealed or painted to match the original moulding. However, in some cases, it looks fine if the build-up is painted plain black.

Round and oval frames can be built up by adding a series of 10mm moulding off-cuts around the back of the frame at intervals of a few centimetres. The back board can be placed over these and the edges disguised with tape.

Glazing

Glazing, which may be glass or plastic, plays an important role in protecting textiles from dirt, atmospheric pollutants, infestation by insects, mould and UV light. Stitches look unattractive if flattened against glazing and the framing looks amateur. Air must be allowed to circulate, so mounts, spacers and fillets must be used between artwork and glazing.

Glazing attracts moisture when there are changes of temperature, such as at night; the temperature inside the frame changes at a different rate, and moisture can collect on the underside of the glazing. If the fabric is distanced from the glazing then this moisture will evaporate causing no harm, but if the fabric or threads are touching it, or there is insufficient space, the damp will be transmitted to the fabric and cause decay.

Fabrics need room to breathe if they are to stay healthy. It used to be con-

This Thai embroidery has a small border of black cotton that was folded around the edges of a piece of 10mm foam board and attached with T-pins. The artwork was not properly square and the T-pins meant that adjustments could be made. A deep wide black and gold frame was chosen to reflect the richness of the piece and foam board was used as a spacer. Once this was hand-painted and sponged it disappeared into the frame.

sidered inadvisable to glaze needlepoint sewn with wool as this prevented the wool from breathing; however, in the modern world the threats to fabric art from our polluted environment are generally considered more dangerous than the use of glazing, so glazing is much more common. It is much easier to clean glazing than to clean needlepoint.

If windowmounts have been used glazing is essential, as the board would quickly become dirty and look shoddy if left unprotected.

Glazing that filters out a high percentage of damaging UV light rays is advisable when framing to Museum and Conservation Levels. However, it should be noted that, while this is recommended, it does not block out 100 per cent of damaging rays, so artwork should still be hung out of direct sunlight.

New generation 'invisible' glazing looks very professional and greatly flatters artwork. It can be almost impossible to detect that artwork is glazed and the cost, as a percentage of the whole framing job, is not significant. Dust and marks can show up more on specialist glass than on ordinary glass, but this does not outweigh its advantages.

Acrylic domes can be used instead of glazing when framing 3D items. These ensure that the glazing does not touch the artwork and mean that it is not necessary to make a box-frame. However, these are only available in a limited range of sizes and shapes.

Caring for framed fabric art

Framed fabrics should ideally be hung in dry, dust-free environments and extreme changes of temperature should be avoided. The main threats to well-framed textiles are discussed below. Frames should be inspected every five years to check that they are still offering the required level of protection.

1) Light

Textiles should not be hung facing windows or with lights shining directly onto them. Light fades colours and weakens fibres causing them to turn yellow, become brittle and eventually turn to dust. Silk is particularly vulnerable to light damage.

2) Swings in temperature and humidity

Do not hang fabrics in damp rooms. Relative humidity should be constant, as radical changes in temperature can cause damage, and should ideally be between 40 and 60 per cent. Mould and insect infestation can set in if the atmosphere is too damp, and colours may start to run. Damp can cause rust-

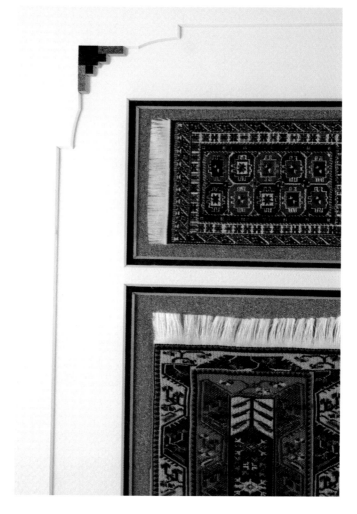

The Turkish silk rugs were stuck onto gold mountboard with EVA, then a multi-aperture double mount was cut. Glue enabled the fringes of the carpets to be evenly presented. The top mount was cut with curves and straights to represent eastern design. Small pieces of mountboard were cut and glued into the corners to pull all the colours together and a muted silver/gold frame was used.

coloured stains to appear on cotton and linen and in extreme cases it causes watermarks.

Textiles are more likely to ripple, and even tear, if humidity is not constant. This is a further reason not to hang them above radiators. Threads contain moisture, so expand and contract as levels of moisture in the atmosphere change. Fibres may expand at different rates, according to their make-up and thickness, which may exacerbate this problem.

Swings in temperature and humidity can be a problem in semi-tropical countries, where the summers are hot and the winters are cool.

3) Insufficient moisture

Conversely, do not hang fabrics in very dry conditions or above radiators. Materials may shrink and become dried out if there is insufficient moisture in the air. They lose their elasticity and so may become brittle and break. Wool is particularly vulnerable; it is designed to keep animals warm in cold weather and can absorb up to one third of its own weight in water, even when spun, so it is not designed to withstand a lack of moisture.

chapter three
squaring needlepoint

Most hand-sewn needlepoint will require squaring, as it will have formed a parallelogram as it was stitched. Squaring is the process of pulling needlepoint back into shape. This process is called 'blocking' in the USA, or 'steam blocking' if steam is used.

1) Why squaring is necessary
Needlepoint is worked on canvas with horizontal and vertical woven threads, which are generally made from cotton. This weave is coarse and loose and needs to be stiffened with size to keep it in place during sewing.

   Canvas loses its shape as heat and moisture from the stitcher's hands soften the size, making it pliable. The canvas is pulled and pushed during sewing and the size becomes wet and dry throughout the process, setting in a slightly different position each time. Unless the item was sewn on a frame, which it rarely is, some squaring is normally required. Most right-handed needleworkers start their stitches bottom left, finishing top right, which means that the canvas will be pushed out of shape in this direction.

This textile by Karen Hall is stitched onto layers of handmade paper. These are hinged onto a conservation under-mount with gummed paper tape. The wide mount includes a V-groove and foam board fillets.

Only attempt to square needlepoint on canvas mesh that has been treated with size. If other types of needlework, such as cross stitch, are out of shape the problem lies elsewhere and will not be resolved by squaring.

A needlepoint may look pretty much square but, if you try holding a set square or a corner piece of mountboard against it, you will often be surprised by how out of square it actually is. Alternatively, assuming the opposite sides are even, measure across the diameters to check for even measurement. A 30x30cm piece can easily be as much as 1cm out of line without the discrepancy being obvious; however, once you put it in a square frame the problem will jump out at you, so you must check the shape before framing.

Any framer who handles a lot of needlepoint will report that standards of sewing vary enormously. Some canvases are horribly distorted by uneven tension during sewing, while others are beautifully even and barely require squaring. The different types of canvas, stitching, stitch sizes and the needleworker's methods of sewing all affect the ease with which squaring can be accomplished. For example, some needleworkers have a heavy hand and pull

This mixed-media Indian textile is surrounded by a neutral multi-aperture mount, then a further top mount lies above a gold beaded wooden slip. A bright ribbed gold frame with a beaded sight edge finishes off the piece

the stitches very tight; if this is combined with a 40 hole per inch petit point canvas the item will be time-consuming to square. Any piece that has been worked by more than one person may be problematic as everyone sews to a different tension.

The fibres must be pushed back into shape, often with the aid of water or steam applied to the back, then held firmly in the desired shape until it is dry. Work that is badly out of shape may need to be squared several times, or at least twice, i.e., once in each direction. The process can take up to a week, as the canvas should be allowed to dry thoroughly between each bout of squaring.

If the artwork is to be laced then it will need to be squared first, as lacing does not allow the fabric to be pulled tightly. If a piece of needlepoint is well squared it will be much quicker and easier to stretch, so it can be worth investing the time and effort at this stage.

Squaring also allows maximum image size: the edges of an out-of-square piece are often concealed by a frame in order to give the appearance of a square.

2) Water, steam or neither

Canvas becomes pliable as it absorbs water, though if it is only slightly out of shape and feels elastic it may be possible to just pull it into square. However, there is a danger of over-tensioning if an item is not pre-squared, as there is a tendency to pull it very tight when stretching. All needlepoint benefits from squaring with steam or water, even if it has retained its shape; squaring gives the stitches a consistent, even appearance and restores the fullness of the threads. If the piece has not actually lost its shape you will not need to spend long squaring it.

Whether you square with water or steam is down to personal preference. Any method of damping can be risky and may cause colours to bleed and wool to shrink, so you must proceed with caution.

You can steam with a kettle, an iron or a steam cleaner. Hold the steaming apparatus at a safe distance and work in short blasts. Some framers like to wear thick gloves to protect their hands from burns when steaming; choose a pair with a good grip and which are sufficiently thick not to distort in the heat. Other framers argue that you are using too much steam and holding your steamer too close to the needlepoint if you find gloves necessary.

Some people prefer to apply water with the type of hand-held spray can that you buy in garden centres for spraying plants. Other people apply water with a sponge.

Whether working with steam or water, take care not to damp the needle-point more than is strictly necessary. Remember that you are softening the size, not washing the canvas. Bear in mind what an over-washed jumper looks like: you don't want the needlepoint to go all 'furry' or 'fluffed up'.

It is safest to work at the back so that the front of the needlepoint is hardly damped at all. However, some framers prefer to work from the front as they feel that the stitches are lifted and refreshed by this method. There is a danger of the stitches fluffing up unattractively if you work from the front, so only adopt this method if you really know what you are doing.

Whichever method you use, you should always use distilled or de-ionised water. If only part of the needlepoint is damped there is a greater risk of brown stains appearing, as soluble salts, dyes and dressing migrate, dissolve and dry at different rates. It is therefore best to ensure that the needlepoint is uniformly dampened.

Many framers ask customers to sign a form acknowledging that they are happy for the framer to treat their needlepoint with water or steam, which is a good idea in our increasingly litigious age.

3) Canvas

The size of the work is determined by the canvas count, or threads and holes per inch, and this can vary from fine petit point single thread to coarse double thread rug canvas. Canvas sizes can range from a count of 4 up to 40; 'gros point' has a count of less than 16, while anything with a count of more than 16

The vibrant mount reflects the colours and Peruvian design of this work by Rhoda Nevins.
A quadruple mount was cut with 'two step long corners' on each mount and a spacer below
to give a shadow effect. The simple pale wood frame reflects the colour of the backcloth.

is called 'petit point'. Needlepoint should be sewn with a blunt-ended needle
to avoid piercing the canvas, which would cause tearing or fraying.

Plastic canvas is becoming more common these days. This should retain
its shape during sewing, but it too will be refreshed by squaring with steam
or water.

There are three main types of canvas:

a) Single or mono weave

This is a simple over-and-under mesh. It is durable and easy to square. The
main problem is with unravelling, particularly in the case of gros point.

b) Double, duo or penelope weave

Parallel pairs of canvas strand are meshed together. The strands are generally finer than those used in single weave canvases, though the whole is
strong.

c) Interlocking weave

This is similar to single weave except that an additional thin strand runs over
each 'junction' to hold the strands in place. This extra strand prevents unravelling though the whole is weaker than the other two types, so must be
squared gently and carefully.

Problems that will not be solved by squaring

1) Edges of unequal length
Measure the edges of the stiched area and check that they are of equal length. If the bottom is 1cm wider than the top, for example, the item will never form a square.

2) Different types of stitches
Stitches of varying sizes and types, maybe sewn in different types of thread and in different directions, cannot be made to form a square. The varying tensions will never form an even shape.

3) Stitches that are not parallel with the weave
If the stitching does not run parallel with the weave, it will be impossible to straighten both the stitching and the canvas. In this instance, most people would prefer the stitching to be in line with the edges of the frame or windowmount.

4) Pucker marks
Pucker marks may occur because of the differing tensions between adjoining stitch types. They cannot be eradicated, though they can be disguised to some extent by padding.

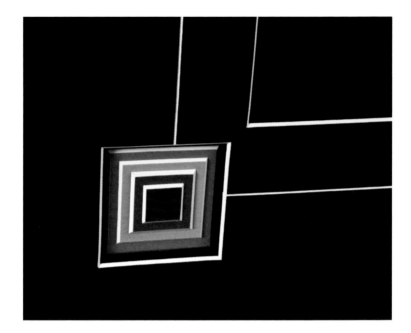

This English gold work was embroidered by Rhoda Nevins onto velvet using gold and silver threads and some areas were padded with carpet felt. The top mount, in black suedette board, incorporates open squares in the corners which are joined together with a V-groove running through the centre. The aperture was cut straight rather than bevelled. Further black, gold and dark blue mounts are used, plus squares of board stuck beneath each of the corner squares.

5) Incomplete rows of stitches

If some rows of stitches have been left incomplete at the ends, the stitches will never follow the vertical and horizontal rows of the weave so will never form a square. The only solution is to hide the 'jagged' edges: for example, by concealing them under a windowmount.

6) Borders

Stitchers sometimes sew borders around their work that they wish to be visible and run parallel to the lines of the frame. If the borders are of a different fabric to the main piece, which they often are, it can be very hard to tension the piece and make it form a square. This problem is particularly severe if a limp piece of canvas is surrounded by a border of a stronger material. All you can do is convince yourself, or the stitcher, that this asymmetry is part of the charm of the item.

Colourfastness

Always start by testing the threads and canvas for colourfastness; you should avoid squaring with water or steam if there is a possibility of the colours running. There are two areas to consider:

1) The threads

Even threads in ready-to-use kits can run when damped, though the instructions may not warn of this possibility. Test small samples of each thread with a cotton bud and distilled water; be sure to rub them hard against a clean white towel, and leave them damp for a while to see if the colours run after time. It does not follow that because one thread is colourfast they all are; they may have come from different sources, so each colour should be tested.

Wool is sometimes dyed using water-soluble sugar dyes; the sugar crystallises, so the colours may not run instantly if the item becomes wet, which may deceive you into believing that they are colourfast, though they will in fact run once the crystals have dissolved.

Ethnic threads should be treated with particular caution as these are often dyed using hand-made colours that have not been chemically fixed.

2) Painted canvas designs

These are generally created with oil-soluble paints, so can be safely damped. However, you cannot guarantee that this is the case and, particularly if the kit is from a supplier you are not familiar with, you must test it before damping.

Rhoda Nevins created this appliqué embroidery using scraps of fabric, beads and handmade cords padded with carpet and craft felt. A small double mount was chosen to reflect colours in the embroidery. Depth is achieved by placing several pieces of foam board under the mount, then lining the edges to hide them.

Also, stitchers sometimes touch up or alter canvas designs themselves using different paints. If you are in any doubt about the quality of the paint then test it before proceeding.

Four types of squaring apparatus

1) Commercial squarers

There are several squaring frames on the market, which are available from framing wholesalers. These tend to be easily adjustable, do not mark the needlepoint and are intended to save time. They can be particularly useful if the item is drastically out of square. Squarers are designed to accommodate artwork of different sizes.

Commercial squaring frames take the strain off your wrists and thumbs, which can be important if you are doing a lot of this type of work.

These sturdy frameworks have rows of 'teeth' to hold the work in place, and a handle that you turn to achieve the correct tension. Once the needlepoint has dried you generally need to turn the canvas round and repeat the process for the other two sides.

2) Pre-marked chipboard or plywood

This type of squaring frame is made by cutting a piece of 6mm chipboard or seven-ply plywood to the desired size, then marking it with a grid pattern. A 60cm square board should accommodate most needlepoint. Be sure to use low density chipboard, i.e., chipboard with loosely packed fibres, as you will be repeatedly pulling out staples or pins.

Plywood is strong and soft, so is easy to work with, and it has a smooth finish. However, it is made from layers of veneer that are joined with adhesive and it attracts bugs and woodworm; it also bows in the heat and in response to changes in temperature.

The centres of all four sides should be clearly marked on your grid. Use a water-resistant marker and coat the board with several layers of yacht varnish when you have finished. A well marked piece of board may be re-used for many years.

When squaring over board some framers cover it with clean plastic. This both protects the fabric from impurities in the board and prevents the board becoming damp, which might cause decay to set in which could damage fabrics squared in the future. However, unless transparent plastic is used this means that you cannot align the fabric to a grid, so you would have to assess squareness with a set square.

The needlepoint should be secured in position with thick-headed pins, such as mapping pins. Staples are not recommended as they can easily damage the fabric; it is hard to control the process of inserting them, and pulling them out can also cause damage. Gently tapping thick-headed pins into carefully selected positions is the preferred method and pulling them out can be a carefully controlled process.

People who do use staples for squaring inexpensive needlepoint insert these with a staple gun. Be sure to adjust the pressure of the gun so that the staples are not embedded too deeply into the board. Staples should be posi-tioned diagonally across both the warp and the weft, so that each staple covers the maximum number of threads. You should not use this method for canvases with thin or fragile strands.

3) Hardboard and pegs

This method involves a piece of hardboard, 3mm or thicker, over which needlepoint is secured with clothes pegs. It is not suitable for stiff needlepoint as clothes pegs are not sufficiently strong.

A great advantage is that it is easy to re-adjust the clothes pegs, which is useful for fine canvas where you need to adjust the tension gently and gradu-ally. The hardboard should be larger than the stitched area so that the pegs only touch the spare canvas and not the stitched area, as they may mark it and flatten the weave. This method is inappropriate if there are narrow borders on the needlepoint, as clothes pegs have quite a long 'reach'. The size to which you cut the hardboard depends upon the amount of spare canvas. It is some-

This tiny piece by Karen Hall incorporates hand-stitching, beading and gold bugle beads. The textile was glued onto board with EVA and then a triple mount was cut. The top mount was 2000 microns thick and the other two green mounts were normal thickness. A gold slip was cut to fit beneath the top green mount. On reflection, the inner bevel should perhaps have been painted gold so that it was not so obvious but it can wait for another day. A Moroccan inlaid frame discovered at a boot fair finished off the final effect.

times useful to modify the clothes pegs (for example, the inside back can be cut out to give the pegs a greater reach).

4) Timber stretcher bars

You can use the same type of stretcher bars that you would when framing an oil painting. The needlepoint is tacked to the sides of the bars with galvanised or rust-free tacks. Some people prefer this method as it allows continued access to the back of the needlepoint, so it can be easily re-damped and then adjusted. You can alter the tension by moving the wedges in the corners or the tacks, depending upon the degree of change required. This method allows maximum air circulation so bulky pieces can dry thoroughly and evenly. However, large pieces of needlepoint may sag or bow in the middle if squared in this way, as the centre is unsupported, so it is sometimes necessary to repeat the process with minimal water or steam. People who frame a lot of oil paintings on canvas tend to feel comfortable using this method of squaring.

How to square

It would be misleading to give precise instructions about squaring. Methods vary according to the type of squaring apparatus used, and framers tend to evolve techniques that fit in with their workshop practices and particular skills. Here are some guidelines.

Opinion varies as to whether to damp before attaching the needlepoint to the squaring apparatus, to damp as you attach it or to damp once it is firmly in place. The choice is largely down to which type of apparatus you use (for example, when squaring on stretcher bars or a commercial frame some people prefer to attach the canvas while it is dry, as it is easier to handle in this state).

If the piece has bulky knots and threads on the back and you are squaring it over board it is sensible to square it face-down so that bumps do not develop which would show on the face of the work.

The work may come into square fairly quickly or it may be a long process; the answer is to test it at intervals, pulling it diagonally and laterally. If necessary, proceed by working the water well into the needlepoint with your fingers so that both the canvas and the stitching become uniformly damp and the work becomes pliable.

Many framers start by aligning and securing a point at the centre of each of the four sides, then adding additional staples, pegs or tacks, depending upon their chosen method. The 'ABCD' method is also popular. The top left corner of the needlepoint is 'A'; top right is 'B'; bottom right is 'C'; bottom left is 'D'. Begin by damping the whole needlepoint, then line up A and B horizontally and secure in position. Lightly damp again, then line up B to C vertically and secure. Damp again before repeating the process for the D to C horizontal line, then the D to A vertical line. Finally damp the whole thing again and leave to dry.

It may be necessary to exert quite a bit of pressure when pulling the canvas into shape; most modern needlepoint canvas is strong and can withstand being tugged and pulled.

Continue damping and pulling the canvas into shape until the warp and weft are vertical and horizontal. It can be a good idea to slightly 'over square' needlepoint that is severely out of shape. This means that the canvas ends up slanting in the opposite direction to the one in which it was out of square, so that, if it slips back when it is released, it should end up how you want it. It should not be necessary to 'over square' by more than 3mm to 6mm, depending on size.

Leave the needlepoint to dry for around 12 hours, until the work has taken up 'permanent set'. Some framers leave it on its squarer for several days until it has fully dried out. It is essential that the work is allowed to air dry thoroughly before framing; if needlepoint is framed while it is still damp it may start to rot and condensation may form on the inside of the glass.

If the needlepoint does not form a square when removed from its squarer, or the warp and weft are not straight, do not worry. It is quite acceptable to carry out the whole process again; it can be necessary to square a piece of needlepoint three or four times. To maximise the effect of each squaring you should let the item dry out thoroughly before starting again.

The sides of the needlepoint should be parallel once you have finished, but they may be wavy due to the pull of the staples, pegs or tacks. The more of these that you insert, the less likely it is that the edges will be wavy. If the problem is not severe the edges will be levelled during stretching.

Needlepoint that has been squared but not yet stretched is liable to revert to being a parallelogram if it is stored in even slightly damp conditions. It is sensible to frame the work as soon as it is thoroughly dry, so you can be sure that it will not drift out of shape and make a second bout of squaring necessary.

chapter four
stretching fabric art

'Stretching' refers to the process of attaching fabric art to a board or framework, so that it is held in shape, before encasing it in a frame. Some methods of stretching are much quicker than others, but the quickest may not be appropriate for delicate or collectable artwork. Framers charge more for labour-intensive specialist methods of stretching. All fabric art must be stretched before it is framed, while only hand-sewn needlepoint needs to be squared.

There are several decisions to make before you start stretching:
1) Which type of support is appropriate
2) How best to secure the textile to its support
3) Consider presentation: for example, whether padding or a sheet of coloured mountboard under the fabric would improve its appearance
4) Does the fabric require extra support, fabric extensions or other special treatment?

It is helpful to have a set square to hand while stretching so you can continually assess squareness and check that the weave will run parallel to the lines of the windowmount or frame. Some people cut the windowmount or frame to size once they have cut the support and use this to check squareness; however, this method is less accurate than the set square, and the windowmount can get damaged. If your support is properly square this is a good guide and makes stretching much easier, but additional checks for squareness are always a good precaution. It is important to check the squareness one last time before you complete the stretching process.

It is essential that the weave of the textile is straight once the fabric is stretched. If the threads do not run parallel to the edges of the mount or frame, the item will look very unsatisfactory.

Before you start stretching the fabric it is a good idea to mark the centre of each outer edge and the centre of the support in pencil so that you can align the two correctly.

You must never cut fabric at the rear to form 45 degree mitres; always overlap it neatly at the corners. If necessary, excess fabric can be held in place by extra pins or stitches. A ruler can be used to push the fabric firmly in place and facilitate neat, tight corners.

There are two main ways of finishing corners. The first involves pushing the two right-angles of fabric together at a diagonal, so that a pleat of fabric is left sticking up, which can be flattened down to form a kite-shaped flap. The second method involves folding one side of the fabric over the support all the way to the edge, then folding the second side up and over it, to form a neat square folded corner.

Achieving the correct tension

The correct tension will vary from item to item; the fabric should be just taut enough not to buckle or sag but should not be pulled out of shape. You must be sure that the tension will not cause the fabric to rip as the fibres expand and contract. It is important that the fabric is stretched evenly around all four edges.

You may find that a fabric looks fine when it is first framed, but that wrinkles appear over the next few days. This may be the result of over-tensioning or uneven tension: fibres are elastic so will relax slightly after stretching.

Lacing (see below) accommodates shrinkage as the materials used should match those of the fabric being stretched, so that they will react similarly to climatic changes and the passing of time. Carpet tape and staples have the advantage of strength but are both unyielding, making it particularly hard to achieve the correct tension, so these methods are not recommended.

A word of warning: when stretching thin silks or cottons the tension may cause 'stress marks' in the form of light and dark stripes. These should be treated with caution and not pulled too tight. You should never staple thin silks or cottons.

Methods of securing fabric art to its support

There are many methods of securing fabric art to its support, each with its pros and cons. Some people are appalled at the idea of using staples or adhesive, while others say that lacing is too time-consuming.

If the artwork is valuable it should be fixed to its support by sewing, or a similarly gentle non-invasive method. The Fine Art Trade Guild's Five Levels of Framing clearly state that adhesive and staples are unacceptable at Museum and Conservation Levels. At Commended Level it is acceptable to attach artwork using fully reversible pH neutral water-based adhesive, but only on washable fabrics. Dry mounting, which involves covering the whole of the back of the artwork with adhesive, is only allowed at Budget and Minimum Levels and is not good practice as it can be almost impossible to remove the textile without damage.

Which ever method you choose, be sure to work over a clean towel or board.

a) Sewing or lacing

This method is acceptable at Museum and Conservation Levels and is the technique preferred by most specialist fabric framers. It allows for re-adjustments throughout the stretching process, so you can ensure that the stitches or weave will run parallel to the mount or frame. Lacing also gives you maximum control over tension and allows the materials to move gently over time without risking damage. Most importantly, it is completely reversible. However, lacing is time-consuming.

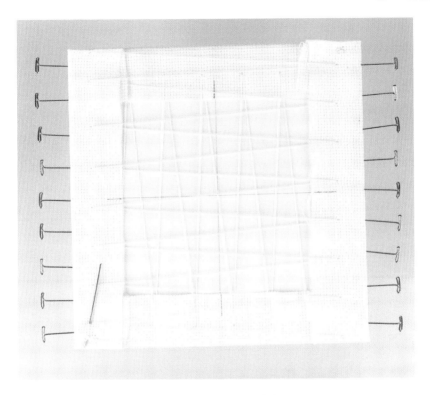

The back of a laced cross stitch

1) Begin by selecting the appropriate needle and thread. It is important that your chosen thread is not heavier than the weave of the fabric as this will generate uneven tension and the fabric may tear. The thread should be less strong than that used in the fabric, so that if undue pressure should be exerted on the framed piece it will be the thread that breaks first, not the artwork. However, it must not be so weak that it will break during tensioning. The type and thickness of thread will vary according to the fabric being sewn.

Crochet cotton is a good average thread for sewing aida cloth, even weave and canvas. Nylon thread is not recommended as it weakens with age, becomes brittle and eventually fails. Framers who specialise in fabric art tend to keep a wide array of threads in stock, covering a range of thicknesses, types and colours.

If the fabric is fine and closely woven and you will be using a thin thread, you should select a sharp needle that will cleanly pierce the fabric. If the weave of the fabric is loose or you are lacing canvas you should use a ballpoint needle that will push the fibres aside and not pierce them.

Do not cut a length of thread before you start, as you do not know how much you will need. Keep the thread on the reel until you have finished lacing each side.

2) Place your support face-up on the workbench; then position the fabric over it. Align the centre of the image with the centre of the support and lightly mark these points on both items.

3) You can hold the fabric in place by sticking a few pins along the outside edges of the support; these should only go lightly into the support, as they should be removed as soon as possible so that they do not interfere with the tension of the lacing.

4) Some framers start by lacing the long sides together; others prefer to start with the short sides. Begin by inserting the needle into the outer edge of the spare border and pull enough thread through the fabric to lace up and down about six times.

   Most framers sew about 25mm in from the edge, depending on the size of the item. The closer together the stitches, the more even the tension. If the laces are sewn too far apart, stress lines may appear on the face of the work. Typically framers allow around 30mm between stitches for large needlepoints, 20mm for medium needlepoints and 10mm for fine cross stitches.

   When the initial length of thread is used up, return to the reel and pull about an arm's length of thread free. Pull this through each insertion in turn to your needle; then continue sewing until the thread is used up. Repeat this process until you are close to the end of the side; then pull the final amount of thread required.

   Continue lacing and gently pulling to the correct tension. Your final lace should be at the corner furthest from the one where you started sewing.

5) Lacing gives you great control over the tension; you can keep making adjustments and do not need to tie off and cut your thread until you are satisfied. You can leave a laced textile for a few days and then check the tension again before finally tying off. Some framers like to temporarily tie off the lace by sewing a small loop around a tiny bit of the border; this loose knot will be undone and re-tied when the tension is right, allowing time to experiment first.

6) Knotting threads is fiddly and they may not hold if you are working on fabric with a loose weave. Instead, 'tie off' the thread by making a loose small stitch and then passing the needle underneath the loop before pulling tight. This can be done several times for security.

7) Repeat the process for the two remaining sides.

b) Gluing

This method is acceptable at Commended Level and below.

   If you are going to use adhesive often, it is cost-effective to buy a big canister and decant it into a smaller, more easily handled container. Be sure to buy water-soluble adhesive, which is reversible.

1) Position the fabric art over the support, mark the centres of the four sides and then secure it with pins or pegs as for lacing.

2) Place the fabric art face-down on a clean soft towel with the support positioned on top.

3) Put a thin line of water-soluble glue along one of the long edges at the
back of the support and then spread this out with your thumb. When the
glue is almost dry, which should take a few minutes, press the fabric onto
it, lining up the threads with the edge of the board. Pegs or pins can be left
in place while the glue dries.

4) Adjust the tension and repeat the process on one of the short sides, i.e., at
right angles to the one already glued. Adjust the tension before repeating
the process on the two remaining sides.

5) The corners should be neatly folded or pleated.

c) Double-sided tape

Double-sided tape can only be used to stretch fabrics at Budget and Minimum
Levels. Many framers refuse to use these inferior materials at all, feeling that
the use of any double-sided tapes for attaching artwork would damage their
reputations and threaten the longevity of the textile.

Carpet tape is heavy-duty, while the tackiness of tapestry tape falls somewhere between normal double-sided tape and carpet tape. Ordinary double-
sided tape can be used to stretch small lightweight items.

The tape should be stuck around the four back edges of the support board
if there is enough spare fabric; if not, it can be stuck on the face though it
should not be behind any part of the fabric that will be visible.

These tapes are strong, easy to use and very sticky, but the adhesive is not
water soluble, so they must not be used to frame items of any value. The bond
will become stronger over time, making the tape hard to remove, and the
adhesive will yellow, thus leaving an unattractive adhesive residue on the
artwork. Eventually the adhesive will dry out and fail.

An advantage of these tapes over glue is that re-positioning is straightforward; when you have found the correct tension, press hard onto the tape, or
burnish it, so that a strong bond is formed. Some people place a sheet of
mountboard over the tape and excess fabric at the back to hold it securely in
place inside the frame. However, these tapes are unyielding once firmly
pressed so it is important not to over-tension the work, as the fabric may tear
as it relaxes.

d) Staples

Staples split threads and are very unyielding so are only suitable for Budget
and Minimum Level framing. As with double-sided tape, many framers would
refuse to use staples at any level and see their use as highly unprofessional.

If you decide to use staples on inexpensive works with a strong weave, you
must proceed with care. You do not have the same control over tension as you
do with other methods; they can tear thin fabric and as coarse needlepoint
canvas has a loose weave it is not possible to get a proper grip with staples

and thus an even tension. It can be hard to align the weave with the edges of the windowmount or frame using staples, as they do not allow for easy re-adjustment.

Even if shallow 6mm staples are used they may show through the work, especially if the pressure on the staple gun is set too high. Be sure to select a good strong board as your support to help reduce this risk, or consider using padding underneath the fabric.

However, stapling can be useful if there are tiny borders and the quality of the artwork does not justify fabric extensions. Stapling is quick and can hold artwork with a medium weave securely in place, so can be useful for budget jobs.

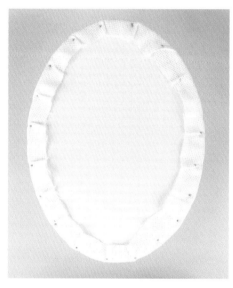

This oval cross stitch is pinned over foam board, then the back is folded into pleats and a few pins are added to hold the spare fabric flat.

e) Pins

Nickel plated pins are acceptable at Budget and Minimum Levels, but stainless steel ones should be used at Conservation and Commended Levels. It is not acceptable to use pins when stretching fabric art at Museum Level.

Pins are used in various methods of stretching fabric art and different sizes should be used according to the type of fabric you are stretching (for example, extremely fine pins are used with silk). The choice of whether to use ballpoint or sharp pins will depend on the weave of the fabric. Inferior quality pins can rust and corrode causing irreparable damage, while stainless steel pins do not corrode.

Some people like to pin small pieces of fabric art on fine fabric, such as cross stitch squares, as pins are easily adjustable, do not require the use of adhesive and hold the item securely in place.

Pinned fabric is stretched over a piece of foam board, so this method is not suitable for large heavy items. The pins are

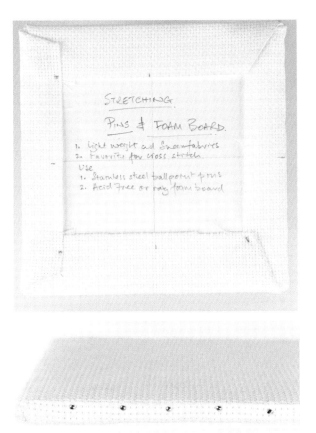

A cross stitch that has been stretched over foam board with pins. A few more pins hold the spare fabric in place at the back.

inserted into the foam sides of the board. Be careful not to over-tension the fabric and cause stress marks.

Start by cutting a piece of foam board 3-4mm smaller than the rebate size. Then position the piece of fabric by lining up the weave with the support, and place pins at the centre of each side, gradually filling in the gaps with more pins and making adjustments as necessary. Only when you are happy that the fabric is straight and the tension is correct should you push the pins in firmly; while you are positioning the fabric the pins can be stuck in loosely. The more pins you use, the more even the tension will be.

The four corners should be neatly folded back; then one pin per corner should be inserted at a diagonal to hold the fabric down.

f) Dry mounting

Dry mounting is only allowed at Budget and Minimum Levels. The back of the artwork is usually covered in adhesive though self-adhesive board (which is discussed later in this chapter) can mean that only the borders are coated in adhesive. Some framers will only dry mount fabrics if an oval windowmount is chosen, as it is very hard to ensure that the weave runs parallel with the edges of the frame.

Dry mounting techniques involve sticking down artwork and fabrics with 'dry' solvents that do not involve the addition of water. Dry mounting can be carried out with spray-on adhesives, self-adhesive boards or tissues that are heat or pressure activated in a press or roller. Reversible dry mounting tissue is available, though reversion can be difficult and time-consuming.

Dry mounting is an acceptable way to flatten and bond low value unstitched fabrics that do not contain wool or 3D embellishments. Dry mounting is a quick method of stretching which ensures that the fabric should end up looking even and flat. It can be useful for thin and poor-quality fabrics that might tear if any other budget method was used. However, there is a chance that the adhesive will soak through thin fabrics and ruin their appearance.

Dry mounting is not suitable for old, valuable or damaged embroideries and fabric art. The pressure required to form a bond would detrimentally squash the stitches in sewn work, so dry mounting is best suited to fabrics such as batiks. Any uneven surfaces will become more noticeable once fabric is dry mounted.

When mounting paper-borne art each of the paper fibres that is pressed down will come into contact with the adhesive; when mounting fabric only those fibres on the top of the weave will come into contact with the adhesive, and therefore the bond may not be sufficient to support the piece. You can sometimes counteract this problem by selecting an extra strong adhesive that is manufactured specifically for supporting fabric art, and be sure to exert sufficient pressure to form a bond.

Bear in mind that the heat from a hot press can cause paint pigments to dry out and crack, so set the press at a low temperature. Waxy batiks may cause problems in hot presses; the wax will prevent bonding, so be sure to remove excess wax before you start.

Some people like to use hot presses as the heat removes creases, rendering pressing unnecessary. Others use self-adhesive board for stretching small items.

Dry mounted fabrics should not be hung above radiators, as the heat will dry out the adhesive, causing it to lose its strength.

g) Hinging

Hinging is acceptable up to Commended Level.

Some lightweight pieces of fabric art on cotton or linen may be hinged to their supports, as when framing works on paper. Small pieces of mixed-media and appliqué work, on which the background fabric has been obscured, can need little stretching, so paper hinges may supply adequate support. Hinges should be made from tape with a water-soluble adhesive, or paper and starch paste.

Lacing and pinning are preferable as they are more secure and no adhesive comes into contact with the fabric. However, paper hinges can be useful when there is little or no spare fabric and the quality of the artwork does not justify fabric extensions.

The artwork is secured by T-hinges at its top edge to the undermount, not the windowmount, as this is more secure. The hinges should be attached to the back of the fabric, never the front.

When hinging artwork on paper, only about 5mm of each hinge should come into contact with the artwork. However, when framing textiles a larger overlap may be required, as adhesion is likely to be less strong as textiles are generally not as flat as paper.

A further horizontal strip of tape or paper should be stuck over the top of the hinge, to secure it to the undermount. The combination of both pieces of tape should form a 'T' shape.

h) Fabrigrip

Fabrigrip is a brand-name for a product made especially for stretching fabric art. This product is suitable up to Commended Level. Fabrigrip comprises lengths of plastic with lines of sharp 'teeth' over which the textile is positioned, so adhesives, pins or staples are not required. However, the teeth may damage fine fabrics so Fabrigrip is best suited to stretching coarse needlepoint. Lengths of Fabrigrip clip on to the edges of pieces of board.

Fabrigrip is useful for stretching needlepoint when a less time-consuming option than lacing is required. It works well with canvas as the spikes are inserted through the holes in the weave, so no threads are broken. Fabrigrip can be positioned onto hardboard or thick mountboard, or a combination of both. Soft-grip clothes pegs can be useful for holding the first two adjacent sides in place while you tension the remaining two sides over the teeth.

Presentation

There are two key areas to consider as part of the stretching process: whether the artwork would be flattered by a sheet of coloured mountboard underneath it or by a layer of padding.

a) Coloured mountboard

A piece of mountboard can be placed between the fabric and the support to form a barrier against impurities in the support (for example, acid in wooden stretcher bars or hardboard). However, this board will not offer total protection as impurities will eventually migrate through it, and the edges of the support will still be in direct contact with the edges of the fabric.

Fabric art on lightweight linen or silk benefits from a layer of mountboard under it, as the colour of the board enhances the colour of the fabric. In some cases it is advisable to use mountboard that is slightly darker than the background material, as loose threads can show up against a bright backing, whereas they would be hidden by a darker one.

If there are a lot of loose threads and travelling stitches you can match the mountboard to these to neutralise them, though this may darken the overall appearance of the work.

Large knots on the back of bulky pieces of needle art can be hidden by cutting small dents in the mountboard in which to rest the knots, thus avoiding the need to use padding. Some framers, however, feel that this practice weakens the board and means that it offers less protection to the artwork.

b) Padding

Bulky knots can be hidden by a layer of padding. Knots at the back may not be visible to begin with, but may appear as bumps at the front of the work over time. Padding can also obscure the puckering which is common on needle art where a section is densely stitched and another left plain, resulting in uneven tension. Padding does not flatter needle art made with thick materials, but it can greatly enhance the appearance of velvets and silks.

Polyester padding is bought off the roll in needlework and craft shops and through some framing wholesalers. It is generally about 25mm thick, so needs to be sliced into thinner layers with dressmakers' scissors. Pieces between 3mm and 6mm are most commonly used.

Polyester padding is chemically inert and so is acceptable for use in conservation framing. Do not use foam rubber as this may start to decay.

The padding should be cut to the rebate size or smaller. It need not be stuck down as it will be held in place by the tensioned fabric. It can be advisable to trim the edges of the padding to a diagonal, especially if a thick layer is used, so that a bulk does not build up, preventing the fabric from pulling evenly over the support.

A thick layer of padding does not look good with a windowmount; it can push against the aperture and cause it to crease. Make sure that the mount is not pressing hard against the fabric; if necessary, place strips of board under the windowmount (see p29 in Chapter 2: Framing).

Ready-stuck padding is available, which comes in varying sizes and thicknesses and is secured to self-adhesive mountboard. While this product is not recommended when framing items of value, it is quick and easy to use and the end results can look very professional.

Curtain interlining material can be used instead of polyester padding to give a more subtly padded appearance.

Fabric extensions

If the fabric art has insufficient borders you can sew strips of similar fabric around the four edges. Backstitch is a good strong stitch for sewing on extensions, though some framers find it too strong and fear it will not 'give' first if pressure is exerted on the textile.

Most machine sewn stitches are not sufficiently elastic, making it hard to achieve the correct tension. However, some framers set their machine to produce a zigzag stitch which should provide enough 'give'.

The fabric of the extension should roughly match the original in weight, but it is better that it should be weaker rather than stronger, so that if undue pressure is exerted on the artwork it will be the extension that suffers.

The width of the extensions will vary according to the amount of extra fabric needed. Some framers overlap the pieces at the corners to ensure that the artwork is protected from strain. Others find this is inflexible and prefer to leave the extensions 'free' at each corner, which makes it easier to achieve the correct tension.

Types of support

a) Mountboard

Mountboard is the most commonly used type of support; 2mm mountboard is sufficiently strong for the majority of fabric framing work and it accommodates pins in the sides quite easily (these are used for positioning the artwork). Some framers find it fiddly to insert pins into 1.5mm mountboard, but use this for lacing small lightweight items. 2.5mm and 3mm mountboard are suitable for supporting larger, heavier items.

Provided cotton museum mountboard is used, mountboard is an acceptable support to use up to Museum Level. Unbuffered board, i.e., board which has not had calcium carbonate added to render it more alkaline, should be used when framing protein-based fibres such as silk and wool to Museum Level, as these require a less alkaline environment than cellulose fibres (such as linen, cotton and paper). Unbuffered boards are specially designed for mounting alkali-sensitive photographs, so can be bought from good framers and framing wholesalers.

1) Once you have cut the board to size it is a good idea to run an emery board or artists' bone over the edges a couple of times to remove sharp edges that might damage the textile and to ensure that the fabric pulls evenly.
2) Place the fabric over the board in roughly the desired position and then hold it up to the light; you can thus see whether the warp and weft are running parallel with the edges of the board and adjust them accordingly. When you are happy with the position insert a T-pin loosely into each edge (if the pins are pushed in too far a dent may appear or the end-papers may tear. The pins will also be harder to re-adjust).
3) Next, lay the pinned artwork on your workbench and place a set square over it. Double-check that the warp and weft are running parallel and adjust the pins until you are satisfied.
4) It can be helpful to score along the line of fabric that you want to position along the outside edge of the board, though this should not be done on work of any value. Take a ballpoint needle and hold this at the end of the desired line; then firmly pull the fabric under it and a scoreline will remain. This will be more accurate than a pencil line as it will follow the weave of the fabric. However, some framers would argue that if the fabric is course enough to take a needle scoreline it should be easy to line up the threads with the support.

5) Attach the fabric art to the mountboard using your chosen method.

b) Foam board

It is acceptable to stretch fabric art over foam board at Conservation Level if the board is faced with conservation grade paper, and at Commended, Budget and Minimum Levels if standard quality foam board is used.

Fabric art can be stretched over foam board using the same methods as for mountboard supports. However, there are three additional methods that can be used when stretching fabric over foam board.

1) Pinning

The fabric is secured to the support with pins, as described in the section entitled 'Pins' on p58. It is not acceptable to stretch fabric with pins at Museum Level.

2) The border, or tight-fit, method

A border of foam board is used to hold the fabric in place. The fabric is secured by the pressure of the two pieces of board, and no pins, staples, adhesive or sewing are required. This method minimises the risk of the fabric being torn or laddered, but is not adequate for artwork on coarse fabric.

This textile is stretched using the border, or tight-fit, method which does not involve any pins or adhesive. The pencil marks enable the framer to replace the centre in its original position, to ensure a good tight fit.

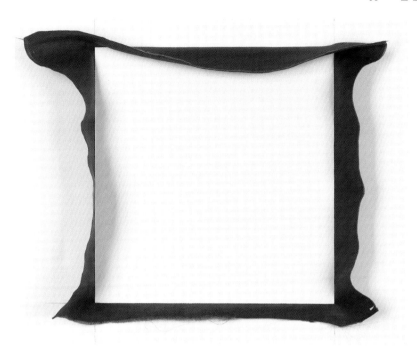

Start by cutting a piece of board 2mm or 3mm smaller than the rebate size depending on the thickness of the material (if this is known at this stage). Then cut the image size from the centre using a sharp razor or similar blade.

Depending upon the thickness of the fabric if may be necessary to trim each inner edge of the border by about 2mm to allow the centre panel to fit back in. It can be a good idea to number the inner edges lightly in pencil so that you can remember which you have trimmed.

Place the border face-down and mark the centers of the four sides; then mark the same four points on both the fabric art and the centre drop-out of the board.

Place the fabric face-down over the back of the border, line up your markings and push the centre down when you are happy with the position.

3) The Newberry Method

This is a combination of the two techniques outlined above. The fabric is secured with T-pins before being placed back inside its border. This technique, and the border method, have the advantages of ensuring that the fabric is held in place and providing a flat surface over which to lay a windowmount.

c) Self-adhesive board

Board with a sticky surface can be suitable for stretching flat fabrics such as silk and cotton at Budget and Minimum Levels. The use of self-adhesive board is a method of dry mounting, which is discussed in the section entitled 'Dry mounting', p59.

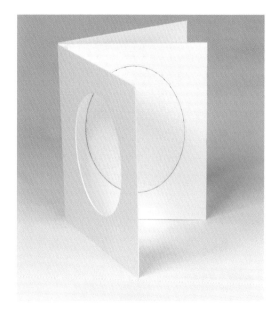

This cross stitch is stretched by the Newberry method, which means that it is held in place both with pins and close-fitting foam board. The stretched artwork has then been sandwiched between a windowmount and an undermount.

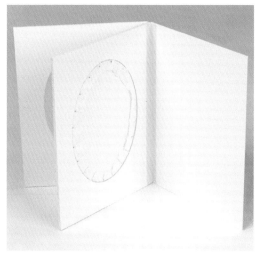

These boards are quick and easy to use; they facilitate re-positioning and allow for maximum image size, which is useful if there is no spare fabric. However, many framers see their use as unprofessional because the artwork or its borders are in direct contact with strong adhesive.

There are two methods of supporting fabric art with self-adhesive board:

1) Complete coverage

This method involves covering the whole of the back of the fabric with adhesive. There is a risk of adhesive soaking through to the front of fine fabrics, so this is a high risk process.

Start by cutting the board to the required size and then peel off the backing paper. Be careful not to touch the adhesive as oil from your hands will be retained and may eventually cause the fabric to bubble and yellow.

Position the fabric onto the board by laying it down gently and then, working from the centre, press in the direction of the fabric grain to eliminate wrinkles and air bubbles.

Once you are happy with the position, press down hard so that a firm bond is achieved. It can be a good idea to place weights on the work to ensure that the bond is strong and that the fabric will not lift off at a later date. Alternatively, some people place the work in their vacuum or heat press at a low temperature. You can also take the precaution of reinforcing the adhesive with staples or tape. Some boards come with silicon release paper to be placed over the artwork to protect it while pressing down on it. It is good practice to use a clean cloth if this is not supplied.

The heat from your hands will activate the adhesive so you should press palms-down, through the barrier layer, before applying weights. Remember not to press hard until you are happy with the position; it is possible to remove the fabric once you have pressed down, but the strength of the adhesive will be weakened and the fabric may be damaged.

Excess fabric should not be trimmed; it should be folded over the back of the board and carefully stuck or sewn down.

2) Borders only

This method means that only the borders of the fabric come into contact with the adhesive. Stretching fabric over self-adhesive board with a padded surface is achieved by this method, as the adhesive is necessarily on the underside of the board.

Begin by cutting the board to the rebate size; then turn it face-down. Next, mark the centres of the four edges on both the fabric and the board.

Cut approximately 25mm from the edges of the release paper with a sharp blade, being careful not to cut the board itself. You will be left with a rectangle of paper in the centre, surrounded by a sticky border.

Position the board on the underside of the fabric with the exposed adhesive facing away from the fabric. You have to do this by holding the item in the air so that the exposed edges are kept clean. It is thus particularly important that the four centres are marked for ease of handling.

When you are happy with the position, fold the borders over and onto the adhesive. This should then be weighted and reinforced if necessary, as above.

d) Hardboard panel

It is only acceptable to stretch fabric art over hardboard at Budget and Minimum Levels, because this type of board is laden with acids that will attack the artwork, even if a barrier layer is used. Hardboard was commonly used as a support for large heavy fabrics before the advent of thick mount-board and foam board, but is much less popular today. However, it does offer a firm support for large needlepoints.

1) Cut a piece of hardboard, with a minimum thickness of 3mm, to the rebate size. Do not use a piece that has previously been used for squaring as this may have been weakened by damp.
2) Round off all the edges, both front and back, using a surform plane or similar tool. The fabric will thus not be damaged by rough edges and will pull smoothly and evenly over the rounded edges.
3) Cut a piece of conservation or cotton museum mountboard to the same size. Lay this over the rough or the smooth surface of the hardboard: the advantage of laying it over the rough side is that the fabric will be pulled

over onto the smooth side, so will slide easily. Others find it easier to position and stick the mountboard to the smooth side. The mountboard layer can be lightly stuck to the hardboard with water-soluble glue, to offer some protection from acids in the hardboard.

4) Lace or glue the fabric art over the hardboard.

e) Timber stretcher bars

Fabric art can be stretched over bars at Commended, Budget and Minimum Levels.

Some people feel that they have maximum control over tension if the fabric is tacked onto stretcher bars and the slack is 'keyed out' using the corner wedges. You can continue to re-adjust the tension by keying out once the item is framed and it will be possible to take it off the wall in years to come and tighten up the wedges. No other method gives such flexibility.

Stretcher bars are the only way to support fabric art that is to have a light shining from behind: for example, painted or dyed pieces (see 'Mounting painted and dyed fabrics that are to be lit from behind', p70). Some stitchers want the back of their work to be visible, in which case stretchers can be the answer.

A disadvantage of stretcher bars is that, especially in the case of work on fine fabric, a shadow may be seen around the edge of the work where the bars press against the fabric. There is also the problem that the migration of dirt is greater at the back of the fabric than under the bars, so a colour difference may eventually emerge. Many people do not realise that work is just as vulnerable from the back as the front, so if you seal the back of the picture thoroughly you can minimise the above problem by keeping out the dust and moisture that attack the work.

A piece of fabric can be tacked to the bars to form an 'under blanket'. An under blanket of lightweight dark cloth can look professional. This layer decreases the chance of a hard line appearing on the fabric caused by the edges of the stretchers. It also hides knots and loose wool, provides some protection against moth infestation and gives a flat uniform surface that supports the fabric while allowing the fibres to breathe.

You can be creative in your choice of under blanket. For example, ordinary canvas can be used and then painted a suitable colour onto which the fabric can be lightly stitched. The edges of the canvas can be left showing, so that the artwork looks as if it is floating.

When using stretcher bars to support fabric art of any value you must protect it from acid in the wood. You can coat the bars with acrylic paint or gesso; three coats should normally be applied and each should be allowed to dry thoroughly before the next is applied. Commercial sealant is not recommended, as spirit-based sealant may be acidic.

You can cover the bars with a layer of strong inexpensive fabric, such as hessian. This can be used instead of paint or gesso, or as well as, in order to prevent the possibility of the fabric art sticking.

The thickness of the stretcher bars limits your choice of moulding, though mouldings with deep rebates are becoming more readily available. However, it is possible to build-up and extend mouldings (see 'Mouldings and build-ups', in Chapter 2: Framing, p35) and it is acceptable to allow the stretchers to stick out behind the moulding by a few millimeters. As long as the back of the frame is securely and neatly sealed this last method does look professional.

Fabric art up to 500x600mm can generally be fitted to standard 45mm timber stretcher pieces of the type used for oils on canvas. It can be best to err on the small side as it is preferable to lose a small bit of the image rather than to have a strip of plain fabric exposed.

Large stretcher bars of around 55mm are often used to support over-sized and heavy pieces, as they are strong and can be reinforced with a number of cross bars. (Cross bars are generally only required when stretcher bars longer than 1m are being used.)

Ideally, wedges will be tied to the stretcher bars with cord or wire, so they do not fall down behind the fabric and cause bumps to appear. You need to drill small holes in the wedges, through which to thread the cord or wire; then attach this to the stretchers with tacks or staples.

1) If you are not using ready-cut stretcher bars, start by cutting the four stretcher pieces to size. These should be cut at a diagonal, then both glued and nailed or stapled together. Assemble the stretcher pieces and then check the right angles using a set square or the grid on a cutting mat or by matching the measurements of the diagonals. Fabric art should be stretched over the bevelled face of the stretcher pieces, otherwise ridges may appear on the front of the canvas as it slackens.

2) Lay a soft clean towel on your workbench and position the fabric art on the support, as above.

3) The fabric should be tacked to the stretchers using 10mm galvanised or copper tacks. Fabric is generally tacked to the sides of the stretchers, not the back, as this gives maximum control over the tension. Start with tacks at centre-top and centre-bottom; then pull out any horizontal slack before putting a tack in each side. Check for squareness before proceeding any further. Repeat the process starting from the left hand side of the first tack, continually checking for squareness. The tacks should be between 25mm and 50mm apart, depending upon size.

4) Corners should be neatly folded and tucked, not cut. Try to keep the folds on the outer edges as flat as possible so that the item can fit snugly into the frame. If the fabric is very bulky it may be necessary to use a liner inside the rebate to allow more space.

5) Any surplus fabric should be neatly tacked down at the back. Make sure that the tacks stay clear of the joins between the stretchers, otherwise you won't be able to key out effectively.

6) Once all the tacks are in place you can adjust the tension by keying out with the corner wedges. To avoid damaging the fabric when keying out with a small hammer, you should insert a small piece of mountboard between the stretcher bar and the back of the stretched fabric. The finished item should be taut but a little movement should be possible. Continue keying out until you are happy with the tension.

7) Finally, attach the wedges with cord or wire.

Mounting painted and dyed fabrics that are to be lit from behind

If you are framing a batik, check that it is not still waxy, as this looks unattractive and is harder to handle. Remove wax by placing the batik between two pieces of brown paper and gently applying a warm iron; as the paper absorbs the wax, replace the sheets.

All materials must be heat resistant so if you are not sure how a material will react to the heat of a bulb, be sure to distance it.

1) Start by mounting the fabric on a timber stretcher frame, as described above. An under blanket should not be used, though the stretchers can be treated with sealant.

2) A sheet of frosted glazing or vellum should be cut to the size of the outer edges of the stretcher bars. This sheet should be screwed behind the stretched fabric and in front of the lights, to both diffuse the light evenly and protect the fabric from the heat of the lights. Vellum is animal hide and is generally sold for making lamp shades.

3) Obtain some thin fluorescent tube lights of a suitable size. These should be protected by pockets of UV-light filtering material and the moulding must be wide enough to conceal them.

4) Choose a moulding with a deep rebate or build a plywood box-frame. This must be deep enough to contain the stretched fabric, glazing or vellum, lighting and the glazing in front of the fabric, if any is used.

5) The components should be assembled and secured with the aid of pins. Back board is not necessary as there is already a sheet of vellum or glazing behind the fabric and it will be necessary to gain access for changing the light bulbs.

Fragile and valuable fabrics

Fragile and valuable fabrics require special treatment and should of course be framed to Museum Level. (See the section on 'Mountboard' under 'Types of support', p63 for a discussion on the best type of mountboard to use when framing protein-based fabrics to Museum Level.)

Below are some key points to remember when working with fragile and valuable fabrics.

This Victorian sampler has been sewn onto the undermount with linen thread going through the old nail holes, leaving the edges visible. The mount decoration leads the eye into the textile and enhances it, yet does not overpower it.

1) Handling and storage

Fragile and valuable textiles should be handled as little as possible. When turning them over, place them between two pieces of cotton museum mount-board and turn the boards over. They should be carefully stored between con-servation quality tissue paper without anything pressing down on them.

2) Donor fabrics

Stitching is the only truly gentle and reversible method of stretching textiles. However, antique items, such as Victorian samplers, may have deteriorated so that the fabric would tear if pulled taut or laced. In such cases you should hand sew the item onto a piece of modern fabric of a similar strength and type, which is called a 'donor fabric'.

All the tension of the stretching process is on this bottom layer. This method is favoured by professional fabric conservators and should be used for museum quality work. If you are in doubt as to the strength of a fabric you should err on the side of caution and use a donor fabric, or pass the work on to a specialist.

It is recommended that you cover your chosen support with the donor fabric, and achieve the correct tension, before pinning, then sewing, the fragile artwork onto it. Therefore any pulling and stretching is done without the vulnerable artwork being at risk. It is advisable to lace the donor fabric in place; in other words, treat it as if it was the textile being framed. Lacing gives you the most control over tension and if the donor fabric is free to expand and contract then there is less chance of any pressure being exerted on the textile itself.

Choose a donor fabric that is similar in type to the old textile so that it will react to the environment in a similar way. However, not all fabrics are pH neutral: for example, silk has a high acid content, so when framing fragile silks it is advisable to use lawn or light cotton as your donor fabric.

The colour of the donor fabric must be considered. In most cases this should match the textile as closely as possible, particularly if the piece is sewn on an open-weave fabric. Moth holes too can be disguised in this way.

A donor cloth can be chosen to emphasise a particular colour. If choosing a donor cloth of a different colour, experiment by laying the textile on a range of colours and see which one has the desired effect. Bear in mind, though, that any holes will be emphasised by a donor cloth that does not match the textile. A solution can be to sew little pieces of fabric the same colour as the textile behind any holes, attaching them to the donor cloth.

Sometimes the edges of the textile are to be left showing, which means that the donor fabric will be visible. In these cases, the donor fabric should complement the textile, but must be sufficiently different to allow the textile to stand out.

If you are framing a lot of old textiles it is a good idea to build up a stock of donor fabrics in a range of weights and types. Shades of beige, cream and off-white are likely to be particularly useful. Experimenting with these will show what a difference your choice can make; one shade may have a deadening effect, while another, very similar, may bring the item to life.

Most fabrics are treated during manufacture to give them body and fix the weave. Donor fabrics should be washed so that dressings are stripped out, leaving the fabric physically stable and chemically inert. Wash the fabric in pure soap, free of colour enhancers, and do not use fabric conditioner or bleach. Rinse it very thoroughly using de-ionised water for the final rinse. The fabric should be ironed on the reverse while it is still slightly damp.

The fragile textile should be sewn in place with thread that is similar in type to the textile itself, but the sewing threads should be weaker. This means that if any tension is placed on the framed item it will be the threads that give way, not the textile itself.

Herringbone is a useful stitch for sewing old textiles in place, which is a loose diagonal cross stitch. However, a simple running stitch may be adequate.

Fine entomological pins can be useful for pinning delicate work in place before sewing, as they will not pierce the threads. (These are pins used for displaying butterflies and insects and can be bought from specialist suppliers.) At the pinning stage you must be particularly careful that the tension is even and the edges of the textile will run parallel to the mount or frame. Pinning the textile in place may be time-consuming and fiddly. However, if you spend time on this part of the process, then the sewing is likely to be quicker.

You then have to carefully sew the artwork in place. A curved needle may be helpful as this enables you to sew onto fabric with board behind. Curved needles and needleholders, which are scissor-shaped pliers that lock onto the needle, can be bought from surgical suppliers.

The amount of stitches required to attach the textile to its support depends upon its weight and type. It may be necessary to support weak or heavy areas with additional stitches.

3) Super-fragile textiles

Textile fibres inevitably lose their strength over time, due to the effects of environmental pollution, light and changes in humidity and temperature. Wool tends to be the most robust fibre as it is the least vulnerable to damp.

Some old textiles were dyed and treated with processes that cause decay to set in over the years. For example, the dark coloured wools in old needlepoints may have been oxidised with iron, which eventually rots the wool fibres. In the late 18th and early 19th centuries manufacturers were experimenting with new chemical dyes which had unknown properties and often caused fabrics to deteriorate. The fashion for 'weighting' silk also causes deterioration; the silk was soaked in tin or iron, which weakens its fibres and makes it even more vulnerable to light damage.

Difficulties arise when fibres have broken down to the extent that they have almost become mineral. They lose their original properties and become dark, hard and crumbly. In a museum environment such fragments would probably be treated with a consolidant, which, in effect, glues together the broken down fibres. However, this is an irreversible process which should only be carried out by an expert.

The safest method of mounting super-fragile textiles is to sandwich them between a donor fabric and a fine, transparent gauze. The gauze should be stitched to the donor fabric just outside the outer edge of the textile. Some immediacy and clarity are lost, but all fragile areas are properly supported and the process is totally reversible.

Items that have been stored folded for many years may split along the fold lines if they are unfolded, so proceed with immense care and hand the item to a conservator if there are any signs of damage occurring. It can be a good idea to support old folds with rows of supporting stitches at either side, which could hopefully be hidden under embroidered areas.

Additional lines of stitching can be added to help position the item further once it has been sewn into place, and take stress off the textile itself. For example, decorations may need extra support or borders and lines that will not lie straight can be gently coaxed into position in this way.

Clothing

Any type of clothing can be framed, the limit is your imagination, though the items which framers see most often are sports shirts and baby clothes. Clothing is often combined with other items within the frame (for example, a cricket cap might be framed along with a ball, stumps and a ticket stub).

Below are some guidelines for framing clothing.

1) Padding

Clothing can be brought to life if lightly stuffed with purpose-made pads or conservation quality tissue paper. This should follow the lines of the item; it both provides shape and prevents the formation of creases. Ready-made pads stuffed with polyester wadding can be bought in haberdashery shops. Alternatively, you can make your own, which can be covered in silk so that the form slips easily into position.

Padding is particularly important for items of value, as creases weaken the fabric, but they look unsightly on any item. Folds will fade unevenly and crush the pile of fabrics such as velvet. The fibres along hard creases may split if they are not lightly padded.

2) Arranging clothing inside the frame

Composition is very important; most items do not look their best if they are just plonked on their undermount. For example, a pair of baby christening shoes should not be framed sitting side by side in a lifeless manner, but should be positioned at a slight angle, as if the child was actually standing in them, or taking a step. You need to experiment to get the best effect.

Most items of clothing can be displayed in a variety of ways; how each item is folded and laid out is down to the owner's personal taste. It is therefore a good idea for framer and customer to agree how the item is to be displayed while the customer is still in the framer's shop. The item should be folded on the counter in front of the customer.

Slippers and shoes can look better if a circle of fabric is inserted into the top, to hide the inside, which may be unattractive. The same fabric should be used for this as for the lining of the box-frame.

Clothing should never be cramped inside a box-frame; items that were intended to be 3D should not be squashed into one-dimensional shapes so that they fit into a frame. Objects need space to breathe aesthetically and they also need to be distanced from the glazing.

If an item was designed to be worn in a particular way, it will probably look its best framed in a similar shape. For example, caps look their best in their intended dome shape and baby bootees look their best rounded into a foot shape. Items that were not intended to be squashed or folded are unlikely to be flattered by that treatment.

Some dresses look their best if they are allowed to hang freely from a hanger, so that the fabric falls naturally. This also reduces the overall thickness of the framing package (folded items are thicker). Chemically inert plastic hangers can be bought from framing wholesalers that are designed for this purpose and come with their own screw to be attached to the undermount and back board.

3) Sports shirts

Plastic 'shapers' can be bought from framing wholesalers that can be inserted into sports shirts to give them shape and soften the folds around the edges. Sports shirts can be folded in various ways; the choice is often dictated by size restrictions and whether logos and signatures need to be visible. It is advisable for the longevity of shirts that they are framed unfolded, so that they fade evenly and hard creases do not develop, but this can make the frame very large. If the shirt is to be folded, you can insert 'sausages' of tissue paper or polyester wadding in the folds to soften them.

The inside of the back of the neck on sports shirts often contains an unsightly manufacturer's label. These can be cut away if the item is of no value but it is not the framer's job to do this, though the framer can suggest it and hand the customer a pair of scissors. An alternative is to cover this label with a club badge.

4) Attaching clothing

When attaching clothing start by placing the item in its final position on the undermount (see the section on 'Undermounts and box linings' in Chapter 2: Framing, p33). Each edge should then be gently lifted and holes should be made with a needle (and thimble!) all the way round. Some framers prefer to use a bradawl for this job, though the holes may end up too large. It is best to make holes from the front to ensure that the position is right.

At Museum Level clothing must be hand-sewn into position and the thread knotted and taped down at the back. Most clothing needs to be sewn all the way round, depending upon its weight, but it is particularly important to sew properly around the top so that the item does not sag revealing unsightly holes.

'Tag guns' can be used to attach clothing at Commended Level and below, and at Conservation Level for items of a coarse or open weave, if care is taken not to break threads. Tag guns are quick and easy to use and can be bought from framing wholesalers. They shoot nylon tags measuring between 4.4mm and 6mm through the fabric and a mountboard or foam board support. Tags come in black or cream, are almost invisible and make a small hole. They can be easily removed if positioned wrongly. If an item is supported by a hanger it can be useful to adjust the drape of the piece with a few tags.

Large and heavy fabrics

If the work is of museum quality you should begin by sewing it onto a donor fabric (see the discussion on donor fabrics under 'Fragile and valuable fabrics', p70). This is also helpful if the piece does not have sufficient borders.

Needlepoint of around 2m wide can be as much as 180mm out of square. Pieces of this size should be squared over plywood as hardboard is not sufficiently strong and may curl, while commercial squarers are too small.

Some people prefer to use stretcher bars for framing large pieces. These must be made from 55mm timber and should have a centre bar as well as additional cross bars, depending upon the size and weight of the artwork.

An alternative to stretchers is 3-6mm plywood, though it is prone to woodworm and can bend in the heat. Be sure to choose untreated plywood. Plywood can be the answer if there are minimal borders, as mounting onto stretcher bars would mean losing some of the image. However, if the fabric is of value you should sew the item onto a donor fabric rather than stretch it over acid-laden plywood. Plywood and other wood-based supports can put the fabric at risk from stains, particularly if they are light in colour. A protective layer under the fabric is advised.

The method you choose for attaching the textile to its support will depend upon its weight, value and rigidity. Heavy-duty Velcro can work well, with one side sewn onto the textile and the other stapled to the support. Tacks and staples can be used for non-valuable items.

The weight of a large needlepoint will be sufficient to give the necessary stretched appearance and the 'nip' inside the rebate of the frame will hold the work in place.

Some large and heavy fabrics will need additional support in the shape of reinforcing loops. This technique is discussed below.

Reinforcing loops

Sometimes large items may require additional support once stretched if they are to lie flat, and 3D embellishments might require localised support. Reinforcing loops can help in both cases. Over-tensioning is not the solution as this could damage the fabric.

Reinforcing loops are particularly useful for fabric with an uneven surface weight, such as Oriental works with build-ups of thick gold thread and semi-precious stones, or coats of arms and collages. Without additional support, these items might billow forward and touch the glazing and over time the fabric might sag and stretch marks may begin to appear.

Loops should be made from thread or thin non-corrosive wire such as fuse wire. Nylon thread is strong, but is fiddly to tie and may yellow and become brittle over time. All thread needs to be tied off, whereas wire is quick to twist and tape down.

If loops are placed at strategic points hidden by the design of the fabric, such as below bulky decoration, they can be invisible. Heavily decorated items over a metre square may require as many as a hundred loops.

Use a bradawl or drill to make holes in your undermount, depending upon the density of the board. Then carefully insert the wire or thread through the holes.

The loops should be around 6mm to 10mm wide. They may need to be re-done once the fabric has settled after stretching, as they may cause it to ruckle or sag.

Rails

Textiles that are heavy enough to hang properly can look attractive if hung from a rail by a supporting tube of fabric.

1) Start by selecting a strong fabric and some corresponding needle and thread.
2) The rail can be made from wood, metal or acrylic. Acrylic is best from a conservation point of view. Cut your rail a few centimeters longer than the width of the fabric art.
3) Cut an oblong piece of fabric that is a few centimeters longer than the artwork and wide enough to generously accommodate the rail once folded into a tube.
4) Fold the fabric in half with the outside facing inwards and then machine sew along the open edge. Turn the tube the right way out.
5) Sew the tube carefully along the top edge of the fabric by hand; be sure to use small stitches so that the tension is even. How close to the top you sew depends upon how much slack there is in the tube and the rigidity of the fabric art. You must allow clearance so that the tube is not visible from the front.
6) The rail must be supported within the frame. This can be done by cutting a U-shaped groove in two lengths of strong spacer and allowing the rail to rest in these. You must first measure the height at which you wish the fabric to hang and cut the spacer accordingly.
7) The spacers should be glued or nailed in place and a 'lid' should be placed over the 'U' so that the rail is held securely in place. The spacers can be painted to tone in with the fabric, or they could be covered in mountboard. Check that the rail fits snugly into the frame and will not fall out of the grooves.

chapter five
projects

These projects are edited versions of articles that first appeared in the leading art and framing trade magazine Art Business Today, *www.artbusinesstoday.co.uk*

Framing a hand-painted silk wedding dress designed by Zandra Rhodes
By Edward Dudfield GCF, 24/7 Art & Framing, *www.bestof.co.uk/evesham*

The dress is suspended from a chemically inert hanger, which is designed specifically for framing clothing. This method of support allows the fabric to hang naturally inside the frame.

I quickly decided that the 120x50cm dress would look best 'free floating' from a coat hanger. This way, the contours, shapes and decoration would be shown off to their best advantage; I didn't want to interfere with the lines of the garment by attaching it to the undermount. I would have to lightly sew the arms in place so that they could be seen properly, but the body of the dress should hang free.

I didn't want the frame to swamp, or compete with, the dress in any way. There is so much decoration on the dress that it was obvious the frame should be understated.

The next step was to measure the depth of the garment. I positioned a long screw in a half-glazed door, and hung the dress on a hanger. It came to life; the full talent of Rhodes was clearly evident as the elegant contours fell into place. The depth of the frills and pearls was 50mm, and I needed to add another 13mm or so for glazing and backing.

Next, I sourced a moulding. I selected a nice little 30mm number made from finished obeche in a shade of distressed, mottled silver. It had to be extended on the reverse with an obeche fillet, as is so often the case, so much of the finish would have to be painted over to ensure a match between the fillet and the rest of the frame. I then chose a cream mountboard to go under the dress and a shade of emulsion for the frame that complemented the mountboard.

The moulding and fillet were cut and glued together with solvent-free Gripfill, but before the adhesive had fully hardened the fillet was pilot-hole drilled and screwed together. I drilled holes first as there was a danger that the wood would split if I tried joining it without pre-drilled holes. The joins were then filled with woodfiller, which was followed by a full sanding.

A basecoat of waterbased primer/undercoat was followed by a lightly stippled coat of 'easy gild' gesso bole. Three coats of emulsion were stippled onto the frame; then a final coat of flat acrylic decorators' varnish was applied, which is my preferred protector.

A piece of 3mm glass was positioned in the frame, then sealed in place with quality self-adhesive tape to keep out thunder flies. The inside of the rebate was lined with a layer of 3mm mount offcuts, then a layer of 1.5mm offcuts, all of which were taped and glued, holding the glass in place.

I did not want to line the box with fabric as I felt this would infringe visually on the dress itself. The subtle light shade of the mountboard coupled with the correct depth of boxing did not interfere visually with the layers of transparent hand-painted silk.

I used a Clear Sports Framing Kit to hang the dress, which is a type of acrylic coat hanger specially designed for framing sports shirts and other clothing. I customised this to meet my requirements. The sides of the hanger were cut down on each side and smoothed, to give a more gentle, feminine curve, more suited to a silk wedding dress than a shirt worn by a burly footballer.

I gave my dad the plastic supporting screw and challenged him to find a more robust steel version (better safe than sorry). A swift foray in his van and he emerged with the perfect item; a screw from a plug socket fitting. I had to cut down the screw thread; then I was ready to attach the dress. The screw was fitted into its holder, and then a nut was attached at the back of the undermount, which holds the hanger in place. The hanger is pressed very tightly against the undermount, so there is no chance of the dress moving or slipping.

I lightly sewed the arms in place, making holes in the undermount with a bradawl and then sewing with a fine cotton thread (I do not trust the metal

T-pins that some framers use). I then fitted the box into the frame, and finished it in the usual way.

Framing a Persian carpet
By Susan J Ilett GCF, Sue's Gallery & Framing,
www.suesgalleryandframing.com

This ornate 2m silk carpet required a simple, slightly distressed, gold frame.

The handmade silk Persian carpet measured nearly 2x1m. The instruction was to frame it with a gold moulding that was not too ornate or bright, and no glazing was to be used. The frame had to be of portrait orientation, because of the nature of the pattern, and the tassels had to be showing. The carpet was heavy, oversize and valuable. The challenge was to frame it while adhering to the principles of conservation.

My customer's parting words were 'Those leather strips can be taken off; they're there to stop the edges curling in transit'. Closer inspection revealed

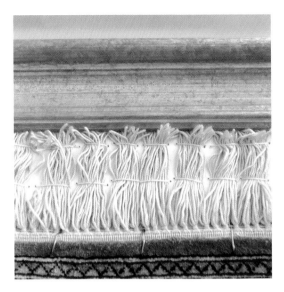

The carpet is attached to the support with loops of gold wire and the tassels are sewn into place with thick cotton.

the strips to be made from top-quality leather which was sewn into the carpet, so would be extremely hard to remove. I wondered if I could utilise them in any way, and decided that I definitely could.

I thought that I would attach the carpet with small lengths of gold craft wire, which I would pass under the leather strips and then into a support at the back. This method would secure the carpet to its support, and would be thoroughly acceptable in terms of conservation as the carpet itself would be untouched.

I decided upon 5mm foam board for the support. This is rigid, lightweight and provides a pH neutral surface for the carpet to lie against. I had to carefully measure the size of the carpet when laid flat with all its tassels straight, and ensure that the support was cut exactly square (which the carpet was not). I initially cut the foam board oversize and marked where the tassels would lie; I then gradually cut the board to size, so that I could be sure I was both cutting square and properly accommodating the carpet.

The gold craft wire was pushed through to the back of the foam board fairly easily; the ends were then twisted together to hold the carpet tightly against its support.

The background colour of the carpet is cream, so white foam board provided a complementary backing shade. I covered the edges of the support with matt gold decorative tape, which concealed the white board and blended in with the sight edge of the frame.

The next job was to secure the top and bottom edges of the carpet to the support. I decided to insert U-shaped pieces of gold craft wire through the carpet, in a series of rings across both edges. I had to take care to balance the need to secure the carpet properly with the need to allow room for it to shift, as it would undoubtedly settle over time. It was thus important not to attach the carpet too tightly.

I had so far enjoyed rising to the challenge whilst seated cross-legged on my floor (the carpet was too big for my workbench). However, the job now became a tussle with the tassels, which were tangled together and quite uneven. I sewed them in place with Perle No 5, a thick cotton of the same colour as the tassels. The tassels were individually sewn to the support in two rows, top and bottom, so that they do not fall away from the support. The top row appears to defy gravity.

I selected a moulding that was big and substantial and sufficiently ornate to complement the majesty of the carpet, but not too heavy, brightly gold or old fashioned. I wanted to ensure that the corner joints were really strong, so I pinned through them at the top edge in the old fashioned way, i.e., with a hammer and nails. I began by drilling holes and cutting off the tops of the moulding pins, then hammered them under the surface and covered them with filler and gilt cream.

The carpet was finally positioned in the frame and a piece of MDF fitted over the back. The latter was secured with framers' points and self-adhesive tape, which is much easier to handle on that scale than tape that needs to be damped with water. Also, the fact that self-adhesive tape does not allow air to circulate so freely did not matter in this case as the frame was un-glazed. I then further reinforced the corner joints with some triangles of MDF, which were nailed over the corners as strengtheners.

The finished frame was not too heavy, since there was no glazing and the support was lightweight. My customer assured me that 50mm brass mirror-plates at each side and top and bottom would be sufficient to secure the frame to his wall.

Framing a large crochet
By Susan J Ilett GCF, Sue's Gallery & Framing,
www.suesgalleryandframing.com

The 80x120cm crochet had the Lord's Prayer worked into it and had taken five years to complete. Because of the size and weight of the piece, and the fact that there were obviously a large number of holes in it, it was badly out of shape. The crochet was going to hang in the local church, which could be quite damp. The frame had to be dark to match the wood of the pews, and the whole job must not be too expensive.

The merits of different types of glass and styrene were discussed, particularly issues of clarity, public safety and weight, not to forget the possible static effect that styrene might have on the crochet itself. It was decided that the church was not so light that non-reflective glass would be essential. In the end they went for standard glass.

Obviously the point of the piece was to have the words of the Lord's Prayer clearly visible, so a black backing that would contrast strongly with the crochet was chosen. I fetched a piece of black mountboard and laid the crochet over it, but, surprisingly, you could not see a word; the black made the

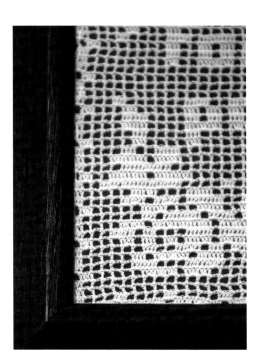

There is no windowmount, but the crochet is distanced from the glazing by spacers which are hidden under the moulding. It is mounted onto sapphire blue suedette mountboard.

crochet seem grey, and the two colours seemed to merge together. Also, the crochet would not hang flat against the mountboard, it just slipped off.

I considered other supports; then suede-covered mountboard came to mind. I hoped that this might provide a surface that the crochet could stick to. I fetched a piece of dark blue suede mountboard as I had no black, and put my theory to the test. Not only did the board hold the crochet but the words contrasted with the board and showed up beautifully. The trouble was that this board is not available in large sheets, so I would have to join two pieces together. However, this would not be too much of a problem as the join would be hidden underneath the crochet. I cut both boards on a bevel and then joined them with tape at the back, before covering the join with a strip of grey-board adhered with PVA glue.

The next challenge was to mount the crochet without stretching and distorting it, thus rendering the text unreadable. I had to wrap the edges around the mountboard and sew it in place, which was quite difficult, and required a lot of patience, as most of the crochet was holes. To do this I used a Perle white cotton, the same gauge as the crochet thread.

The item was to be framed without a windowmount, so I used 5mm strips of clear plastic spacer to separate the crochet from the glass and to allow air to circulate. These strips were invisible as they were hidden by the lip of the moulding. The mounted crochet was then secured into the frame and further protected with an undermount of conservation quality mountboard and a sheet of conservation quality specialist back board. This has a waterproof backing, which would offer some protection against the damp in the church. Finally, triangular pieces of MDF were cut and secured with moulding pins across the corners in order to strengthen them.

Two gentlemen from the church committee, one being an engineer, came to discuss the final hanging of the crochet. I suggested various types of heavy-duty and security fixings, which were mostly dismissed as they involved permanently attaching the crochet to the wall, and planning permission from the diocese is required to do this. They therefore decided to sort out the matter themselves, depending on how much of the red tape they could untangle.

Framing a wedding bouquet of silk flowers
By Peter Cleevely GCF, Picture Corner,
www.picturecorner.co.uk

I decided to keep the frame simple and uncluttered, so the bouquet is surrounded with just a metre of bridal dress fabric and a metre of veil fabric. I didn't want to detract attention from the bouquet; however, you may choose to add the bride's garter, an invitation card, a champagne cork or a plaque engraved with the bride and groom's names and the date of the wedding.

The bouquet measures 52x40x95mm. I cut a box out of conservation quality mountboard that allows the flowers to be surrounded by a flattering border,

The fabric lining the box is deliberately left loose with plenty of folds to achieve a sumptuous look. The silk bouquet nestles in a metre of bridal dress fabric and a metre of veil fabric.

about 50mm on all sides, but doesn't make the box inconveniently large. It is important to choose mountboard in a soft neutral colour that will not alter the colour of the fabric.

Before the sides of the box were folded up, I covered the bottom and sides with double-sided tape, so that the silk bridal gown fabric could be stuck down and held in position. Before positioning the fabric, I folded up the sides and glued the four corners together. When the glue dried I positioned the fabric.

The fabric looks sumptuous left loose with plenty of folds and creases around the walls and at the corners, but it was pressed flat at the bottom of the box where the flowers would lay. When the position of the fabric looked right, I trimmed the outside edges leaving an overlap of about 25mm which was folded over and stuck to the outside of the box with tape (this tape was eventually covered with an outer box).

The veil fabric had to be folded into several layers, so that it had sufficient depth and substance to enhance the overall display. It was folded to the size of the base of the box, and the picture wire that would hold the bouquet in place also secured the veil.

The handle of the bouquet had to be carefully bent round into a 'U' (so that it pointed into the bouquet itself). The bouquet was thus flat at the back and the handle formed a strong anchor so it could be secured to the box with brass wire. I then marked positions for four holes, two at each side of the handle, and punctured holes in the mountboard with a picture pin held in a pair of pliers.

At this stage an extra pair of hands was necessary to hold the netting and flowers in position, as picture wire was threaded over the handle and tied at the back of the board.

I made an 'outer box' from conservation back board, which ensured that the box stayed rigid but remained light in weight. The second box also hid the tape and overlapping silk fabric. The measurements of the outer box are 2mm larger than the inner one, so that the first box slipped snugly inside the second. When the box was cut, folded and glued into position, the first box and the bouquet were gently pushed inside.

To show the fine detail of the flowers and fabric at their best I decided to glaze the frame with 'invisible' non-reflective glass. Choosing the frame was straightforward; a champagne colour would complement the fabrics so I selected a 50mm slightly distressed champagne moulding, which blended in with the high quality of the fabrics whilst at the same time allowing the bouquet to remain the centre of attention.

I double-checked that the glass was perfectly clean, then placed it on top of the box and positioned the frame over it. I then carefully turned over the whole assembly and applied some clear adhesive to seal the frame to the box.

I left the frame to dry overnight, then covered the sides with off-cuts from the silk fabric. I cut the fabric wide enough to fold over onto the back of the frame and under the moulding, to give a neat finish, then attached it with double-sided tape. I used two lengths of fabric, each one covering a long and a short side of the frame. I finally added D-rings and dark brown cord.

This project took no more than two hours to create.

Float-mounting a small fabric onto stretched canvas
By Mal Reynolds GCF Adv, Harlequin Frames,
mal@harlequinframes.f9.co.uk

Anne Menary uses recycled materials wherever possible; her textile pictures are made entirely by hand using a combination of felts, fabrics, paints,

This highly contemporary frame design flatters these fashionable textiles. The artwork is sewn onto canvas that has been painted black, which is then surrounded by deep black mounts and a distressed silver frame.

stitches and applied objects. Her Postcards from a Time Traveller series demonstrates a rather 'other worldly' take on life.

When framing fabric art you must 'think outside the box' and be flexible. It may be necessary to adapt techniques and materials, which is fine so long as your work is reversible and will protect and conserve the artwork. A good understanding of the Guild's Five Levels of Framing helps guide your decision making.

My first thoughts concerned how to support the artwork. I had recently visited a gallery and seen textiles supported on stretched canvas, so I decided to give this a try. I bought a large stretched canvas, then took it off its stretcher bars and cut it in half, as I had two 'postcards' to frame.

I made two stretcher frames slightly larger than the postcards, which allowed for a border around the artwork. I stretched the canvas, pinning it at

the back, then gave it three coats of black paint. I positioned the artwork in the middle of the canvas, then lightly sewed it in place.

I wanted the artwork to 'float' in the frame, so a box frame or deep-rebated moulding was required. However, the moulding that I wanted to use for aesthetic reasons does not have a deep rebate, so I had to opt for a box frame. I had several lengths of L-shaped box moulding machined from knot-free pine by a timber merchant, which was surprisingly inexpensive. This was cut and joined to form the skeleton box.

I then cut a piece of 2mm MDF to fit and glued it to the bottom of the box, which was painted black. I cut pieces of black mountboard to size, which were glued into the base and around the insides of the box.

The next job was to screw the supported artwork and its canvas into the box. I measured the centre points of both canvas and box, and lightly marked these at the back. I drilled a small diameter guide hole through the MDF and the mountboard, and, once I was satisfied with the position, I screwed the canvas in place from the back.

I now turned my attention to the distance between the glass and the artwork. I wanted a 10mm space, which would require a double window-mount. If a windowmount had not been necessary for this reason, I need not have used one as my box-frame moulding was machined to a width that would be hidden behind the lip of a moulding. However, I think that windowmounts look very smart within box-frames.

I cut a double windowmount from black mountboard with a black core, then positioned this against the glass. I chose glass with a UV-filter as well as reduced reflection properties.

The top, silver, moulding was mitred and pinned and the frame was assembled. The box was screwed and pinned to the moulding, and then the frame was neatly taped at the back.

Float-mounting a mixed-media textile and displaying it in a box-frame with hand-decorated mounts
By Mal Reynolds GCF Adv, Harlequin Frames,
mal@harlequinframes.f9.co.uk

The fabric is float mounted over a hand-painted undermount decorated with harlequin diamonds. Diffused glass is used to deliberately blur the diamonds behind the image, leaving those at the front in full focus.

The mixed-media fabric, which depicted a harlequin, was made using a combination of felts, fabrics, paints, stitches and applied objects. I wanted to create a frame that would flatter the delicacy and subtlety of the original, and not overpower it, yet the frame and mount designs should be colourful, in keeping with the harlequin theme.

The textile was to be float-mounted; I would lightly stitch it to its support, then make a box-frame of the required depth. Finally, conservation glass would provide protection from ultra-violet light.

Though this artwork is a step removed from the cross stitch and needlepoint that regularly arrive to be framed, the project covered many of the issues that one has to consider when framing any textile. I firmly believe that the Guild Commended Framer programme, along with its advanced modules, provides the framer with the knowledge, skills and, above all, the confidence required to undertake such projects.

The artwork is A4 in size: in other words, it measures 210x297mm. It needed to be attached to a support in the gentlest possible way, so that there would be no chance of the backing cloth being damaged as the fabrics expanded and contracted over time during the changing seasons. Since it is

made using a range of materials and techniques, the artwork includes various tensions, so I had to be sure that I didn't put any further strain on it when supporting it.

I decided that four light, evenly spaced stitches, both top and bottom, would be sufficient, and that a piece of conservation mountboard would provide the right support. The stitches at the top hold the fabric in place, while the bottom ones prevent it hanging too far forwards and touching the glass. If you hold the finished frame face-down, the artwork sags slightly as it is supported so lightly, but I am happy with this as it means there is definitely sufficient slack to allow the materials to expand and contract over time.

The colour of the conservation board is irrelevant, as it would be entirely hidden. I cut it 15mm smaller than the artwork, and then smoothed the edges down with an artist's bone, so that the artwork would not be lying against sharply cut edges. Using a small drill, I made holes in the mountboard for sewing; I prefer not to use a bradawl, as this can leave holes with jagged edges that might rub against the artwork.

I sewed the artwork in place with a blunt-ended tapestry needle. This type of needle will not damage the threads and fibres of the artwork, as it forces them aside rather than piercing them, which would weaken the artwork.

I used mercerised cotton for the sewing; my policy is to sew fabric art using the same type of thread as that from which the original piece is made. Mercerised cotton is a good option because it is better quality than ordinary sewing thread; it is smooth and lustrous and pulls through easily without knotting or fraying. It is available in needlework shops and comes in a variety of colours and thicknesses. I try to use thread that is slightly finer than the thread used to make the artwork, so that, if any strain at all is put on the mounted artwork, the supporting thread will break before any of the threads that make up the artwork itself.

The stitches were tied off and the ends were taped down at the back with quality self-adhesive tape; this looks neat and ensures that the fabric is held securely in place. I deliberately left the tension quite loose when I sewed, which is a good precaution when working with mixed-media pieces. Again, I would always rather that the artwork sagged forward slightly than that it be placed in any danger.

Next, I cut two pieces of 5mm foam board to the same size as the conservation mountboard support. The two pieces were glued together and, once they were dry, the conservation quality support onto which the artwork was attached was glued to the foam board with aqueous EVA. The three boards combined are about 12mm thick, which raises the artwork above the undermount to provide the desired 'floating' effect.

I needed to ensure that the sides of the 12mm 'sandwich' were hidden. To this end, I cut four strips of black-core mountboard and glued them around the four sides of the sandwich. The artwork still projected slightly beyond all the pieces of board, none of which were visible.

I used off-white textured conservation mountboard for the undermount, spacers and windowmount. I decorated these mounts with harlequin-style diamonds about 50mm square, which I drew lightly in pencil, then coloured with gentle watercolour washes in blue, red, green and yellow, which are the harlequin colours. The supported artwork was then glued to the undermount with EVA.

I needed to make a box frame because the combined depth of the glazing, artwork, boards and backing was greater than the rebate of my chosen moulding. The choice of moulding was difficult, but I finally settled upon a blue-on-silver design, as the colours reflected those in the artwork.

I used ready-made box-frame moulding to build up the sides, which created a box that projected about 25mm beyond the rebate at the back. I ensured that this projection was neatly covered with brown paper tape at the back of the frame.

The box was lined with 5mm foam board, then with the painted mountboard spacers. These linings were taped into position: the top and bottom spacers first, so that the sides would hold them in place should the tape eventually fail. In other words, the top and bottom foam board and decorated mountboard strips ran the full width of the box, while the sides were cut a bit shorter to accommodate the thickness of the first two strips.

A windowmount was required to conceal the edges of the spacers, but I kept this narrow so that there was maximum space around the artwork. I took the trouble to ensure that the diamond pattern on the windowmount was correctly aligned with that on the undermount, so that the pattern appears to be continuous. I did the same with the spacers and the undermount.

I wanted to use glazing that offered a level of protection from damaging UV light, as the vivid colours could be particularly vulnerable to fading, and the various fabrics might deteriorate if exposed to light. I chose diffused glass because I liked the idea of this slightly blurring the diamonds that were painted on the undermount, without it distorting the artwork, which was only 10mm below the glass. It would also leave the pattern on the windowmount distinct. I was very pleased with the result: the way that diffused glass slightly blurs distant images is generally seen as a negative point, but in this case I think I have turned it into a positive asset. People who see the frame, particularly artists, often ask how I created a watercolour wash that fades so subtly into the background; they are amazed when I explain to them that the effect is created by the glass, not with any kind of decorative painting technique.

Finally, the various components were assembled, the frame was taped together, and the hanging fittings and bumpers were attached. The finished frame measures 555x460mm. It hangs in pride of place in my gallery and provides a talking point with customers.

Framing a large Indian mixed media embroidery
By Norman Herringshaw, Herringshaw Framing,
0161 941 6817

Each of the padded shapes in this mixed-media embroidery had to be supported by specially cut cardboard shapes which were sewn into position by hand.

The elephant was a souvenir from a trip to India: a fine fabric image, just over a metre square, with a deep padded elephant in the centre, surrounded by padded horoscope symbols, beads and gold thread. The challenge was to fix these padded shapes so that they did not sink to the bottom of the frame.

I began by making cardboard 'supports' for each padded shape. I laid paper onto the image and traced the outlines of the shapes onto it. I transferred the tracing onto 2000 micron back board, then cut out the shapes with my Rotozip (this tool is a very handy addition to the framer's arsenal).

Next, I drilled a series of holes around each cutout and then fitted passe partout rings into these holes. The use of brass passe partout rings lessens any longterm risk of rusting. Finally, I drilled holes all round the outside of the board, 2 inches from the edge, and fitted passe partout rings into these holes as well.

I spread the fabric image face-down on the table, laid the card on top of it and lined the holes up with the padded shapes. Then, using a curved needle and strong black linen thread, I attached the shapes to the card by passing the needle through the padding, then through the rings and then back into the shapes, until all the rings were looped in and the pad was fixed firmly. I repeated the procedure for each pad, then for the whole image, overlapping the fabric edge and tying it in to the rings.

Finally, I prepared a series of 50mm wide card strips which I glued alongside the surrounding rings with PVA. When these had been dried in place under weights I used them to glue the whole shebang onto the MDF backing. The image was now protected from the acid in the MDF by its own lining and a 4000 micron thickness of card.

For the rest of the project I followed conventional 3D framing principles. The customer had chosen a 50mm black obeche moulding, one of my collection of workshop-stained bare woods. With this went a 75mm bare wood fillet, also stained black, which was deep enough to hold the glass clear of the elephant.

Having cut the glass I set it in place and attached the frame to the fillet with an additional section of black stained obeche. Next, I stapled the MDF to the fillet. I taped the edges with gummed paper tape, and as a final flourish I painted the tape black.

Framing boxing shorts
By Peter Cleevely GCF, Picture Corner,
www.picturecorner.co.uk

The boxing shorts were highly collectable and were signed by Joe Frasier. When framing any irreplaceable object my thoughts go straight to conservation and how to avoid gluing the object to the undermount.

The shorts are attached to the undermount in a way that gives the impression that they are floating in mid-air. The shorts stand slighty proud of their background, and I wanted them to hang cleanly down, without any visible support.

The waistband was stuffed with several pieces of black foam board, which were cut and stuck together to give a 15mm thickness. This provided the shorts with structure and shape. Strips of foam board were also added under the waistband; these were sewn to the shorts, and then the underside was glued to the undermount. The bottoms of the shorts were left hanging freely with strong pleats. These were just gently tacked into place, to position the legs into an aesthetically pleasing shape and to ensure that the signature can be seen.

The box was made from 5mm black foam board. I cut a rectangle on which to position the shorts and lightly scored 15cm margins on all four sides. I cut

The shorts are framed using sloping mounts, which are ideal for framing simple solitary objects. The effect adds interest without looking gimmicky.

the four corners out with a sharp scalpel, so the four sides could be carefully folded upwards and glued. The glue was left to dry overnight. When gluing, always use a mild glue or adhesive; some glues can attack the foam board and weaken it. I like to use a clear silicone, which is clean and easy to apply.

I placed the lightweight yet sturdy box on the bench, then laid the shorts inside and experimented until I was happy that I had found a position that was aesthetically pleasing.

The windowmount was off-white, finished off with a gold innermount. The latter was complemented by a 5cm gold mottled frame.

The depth of the box gave the mounts considerable prominence. I therefore wanted them to do more than just contain the shorts; I wanted them to convey a message of quality framing. I have seen so many framers just put an object in a box frame on its own; I always try to add a higher level of presentation and finish to my work.

I spent ages experimenting with multiple mounts, but each combination still looked standard and everyday. The problem was the simplicity of the object being framed; a radical approach was called for. I stuck at it; I tried placing mounts a third of the way down, three quarters of the way down and directly under the glass. Nothing worked until . . . I had an accident. A mount was taped at one end, allowing the other to fall into the box. I looked at the effect and realised at once that a sloping mount was the answer to my problem. I decided to move away from conventional flat-and-equal spacing, by tipping the mounts at angles. I experimented a bit more and kept letting the mount fall into the box, taking measurements as I went. Eventually, I found a combination of two sloping mounts that was aesthetically appealing and that led the eye into the shorts, rather than overpowering them.

The black undermount slopes from front to back, while the top double mount slopes from back to front. Strips of black foam board were cut to the desired angles; I attached these 'wedges' with double-sided tape to the inner edge of the box, which held the mounts in position.

Sloping mounts are ideal for framing simple solitary objects. The angle of the slope draws in the gaze, but the framer can prevent the mounts from overpowering the object by choosing simple muted colours. Sloping mounts are very much in keeping with today's ideas about mount design: thick, wide mounts are in, while fussy decorated mounts are out. Sloping mounts have an almost trompe d'oeil effect, but without overwhelming the simplicity of the object, and the end result certainly doesn't look gimmicky.

I have developed the theme into a design of fanned sloping mounts. This involves using various thicknesses of foam board, 5mm and 10mm, and placing strips between the mounts to create distance. A subtle combination of maybe two mount colours can be used to stunning effect. The end result looks very different from the vast majority of box frames that you see, and, like most framing methods, the technique becomes quicker and easier to do as you practice.

I have used this idea many times since framing the boxing shorts. I have a framed ring on display in the shop (a fairly plain gold finger ring), which looks fantastic in a range of fanned sloping mounts and has prompted many a customer to opt for this design.

Back to the boxing shorts, I used conservation quality UV-filtering glass, as I wanted to protect the valuable signature and to prevent the shorts from discolouring over time. After cleaning the glass and dusting out the box, the frame was placed over the box and glued into position. To finish, D-rings were screwed into place on the back of the frame. Both the D-rings and a tiny bit of visible glue were painted black, and black cord was added when the paint was dry.

Re-framing a cross stitch that has suffered damage, both physical and aesthetic, from poor framing
By Mal Reynolds GCF Adv, Harlequin Frames,
mal@harlequinframes.f9.co.uk

The cross stitch had been framed some years ago, but my customer wanted the piece re-framed as it has sentimental value and she had never liked the frame. It is a piece of counted cross stitch, made with linen thread on a bleached linen base fabric of approximately 24 count (this means 24 holes per inch).

This cross stitch had previously been framed using harmful acid-laden materials and was visually very cramped. It has been re-framed with wider windowmounts which allow the image room to 'breathe'.

My customer's cross stitch had been badly framed. The design of the frame and mount was poor; the cross stitch looked cramped in a single mount, cut from standard mountboard, which left insufficient space between the work and the glass. There was a real danger that moisture generated by the micro-climate inside the frame might transfer from the inside of the glass to the fabric, causing terrible damage.

After removing the masking tape and back board I found that the work had been cut to size and stuck to poor-quality board using double-sided carpet tape, which was taped over with brown self-adhesive tape. Masking tape is designed for short-term use and has no place in a professional framing work-shop, while cutting work to fit a frame is unacceptable. The framer's job is to preserve work for future generations without altering its original condition, a principle that this framer had totally ignored. All needle art is unique and often has sentimental value, so the cross stitch should never have been framed using these materials and techniques.

After carefully removing the work, I found that the edges of the linen were sticky and beginning to yellow as a result of the residue from the self-adhe-sive tape. The artwork looked slightly dirty, especially the areas that weren't stitched, and there was a small stain, possibly caused by careless handling.

Dirty fabrics contain acid, which in damp or humid conditions may attract mould and insects thereby causing long term damage to the fabric and threads. I suggested that the customer should wash the work to remove the dirt and adhesive residue, which would also return the work to a neutral pH. Framers should not attempt to wash customers' fabric art, as the colours may bleed and shrinkage may occur. It is best to warn customers of these poten-tial problems and let them handle cleaning.

When my customer returned, the appearance of the work was significantly improved. The adhesive residue had gone, other than some slight yellowing of the linen fabric. The small stain was reduced in size and the threads had returned to their vibrant and full texture, which was a great improvement.

After discussing the frame and mount design with the customer, I had to decide how to attach the work. My preferred method of stretching is lacing, but because the previous framer had trimmed the work there was insufficient material for lacing. I needed to achieve the correct tension and stretch the work evenly around all four edges, but the linen was frayed and I was con-cerned that lacing would pull it apart. In the end I opted to (very carefully) pin the textile to the foam board. While this method is not suitable for large or heavy items it is useful for small cross stitches.

I cut a piece of 5mm foam board slightly larger than the aperture of the win-dowmount. In order to correctly align the artwork and its support I marked the centre of each outer edge, on both artwork and support, in pencil, on all four sides. I positioned the fabric onto the support using the marks, lining up the weave and support as best I could.

I then inserted stainless steel ballpoint pins, purchased from the local needlework shop, into the centre of each edge, i.e., into the core of the foam board. Working outwards from each central pin, I placed the rest of the pins about 10mm apart, ensuring that the weave was straight and that the fence post in the design was vertical.

The pins were left sticking out slightly so that I could adjust them, if neces-sary, at the end of the stretching process. I pushed them in firmly when I was happy with the position of the work and the tension. I then folded all four corners neatly and inserted a pin across the diagonal of each corner to hold the fabric down.

Next, I placed the supported work on an undermount of white core mount-board, a few millimetres larger than the work itself. Then I cut four lengths of 5mm foam board that would fit snugly around the artwork and hold it in place, each with an outside edge that was flush with the outside edge of the white core board. The four strips of foam board were then glued into place. These strips would also act as 'fillers' around the work which would ensure that the windowmount lay flat. They did the simple job of 'scaling up' or adding surface area to the piece so that I could give it the larger-scale framing treatment I felt it deserved.

Wide borders of unstitched linen would have looked best, but this was not an option as the edges had been cut away. I managed to leave about 10mm of unstitched fabric around the work. Image size is important; artwork needs room to breathe and should never look cramped in the mount. A good rule of thumb is to leave between 5 and 10 per cent of unstitched fabric visible in the frame, though this depends on the boldness and size of the work and the texture of the stitches.

The double mount was cut from white core and conservation quality mountboard, and hinged along the long side of the supported work. Whilst I would have preferred to use conservation board exclusively, my customer liked the effect of the white core board.

Once assembled, the thickness of the windowmount, supported work and undermount was around 10.5mm. Once the glass and back board were added the depth of the package was greater than that of the rebate of most mouldings, so I decided to make a small box frame. This would also allow me to include spacers to increase the distance between the artwork and the glass.

I constructed a box frame from special box-frame moulding. I placed the artwork and glass inside the box and measured the depth that was available for the spacers. These were cut from 5mm foam board, lined with mountboard. The spacers projected beyond the lip of the moulding, so I had to hide them with a narrow windowmount that was positioned directly against the glass.

A note regarding my choice of glass: since this job was for a regular customer, I knew that she would want glass offering protection from UV light. She mentioned that she intended to hang the work in her office which has fluorescent lighting. Reflection is a problem with fluorescent lighting, but I explained that there could be a loss of definition if I used diffused glass to combat this, because of the distance between the artwork and the glass. This distance, I explained, is necessary to maintain air flow around the work, to prevent threads being crushed against the glass and to prevent the threads and fabric getting damp from condensation, which could generate mould and decay. In the end we decided upon glass which offers UV protection and is 'invisible'.

The glass was cleaned and placed behind the narrow windowmount inside the rebate. Next, the spacers were stuck in place with ATG tape; the top and bottom spacers were stuck in place first, then the side ones. They were positioned in this order so that the side spacers would support the top one if the tape failed.

I then checked the mounted work for loose threads, etc. and placed it into the frame. An MDF back board was secured with framers' points. The finished work was once again checked for dust and blemishes before the box frame was fastened to the moulding with framers' points, and the back was sealed with gummed-paper tape. The outside measurements of the finished frame are 540x460mm.

The original badly designed frame meant that this good piece of cross stitch looked very mediocre. Furthermore, poor framing techniques had damaged the fabric and if it was left in its original frame further deterioration would have undoubtedly occurred. Both backing fabric and threads would have suffered from attack by acids in the inferior framing materials used, damp would have been transmitted from the glass to the artwork, causing mould, and fading and weakening of the threads would have been caused by exposure to UV light.

Re-framing the work transformed it, and my customer agreed that it now had the 'wow' factor. All materials and techniques used in the new frame were fully reversible and would protect, rather than threaten, the artwork.

Framing a multi-layered, highly decorated and heavily embroidered textile
By Lyn Hall GCF Adv, Fringe Arts,
www.fringearts.co.uk

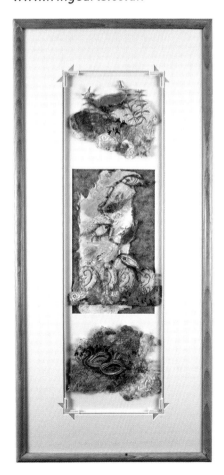

The top and bottom sections of this piece by Linda Chilton are machine embroideries worked on felt and dissolving fabric (certain areas are worked on dissolving fabric so that when washed, the background disappears leaving open work). These two sections are stitched onto mountboard so that all the edges show. The central section is made from handmade paper which is embroidered and embellished. The colours in the mount reflect those in the artwork and the corners are designed to reflect the tail of the fishes. A simple limed oak frame was used because of its neutrality.

Framing mixed-media textiles is unlikely to be straightforward. Artwork that is lumpy and uneven and incorporates a range of fabrics and other materials, all with different properties and of varying tensions, can cause even experienced hands to hesitate. Such works require extreme care but, with patience, creative thinking and a multi-disciplinary approach, successful and lasting framing solutions can be found.

I have framed the works of textile artist Linda Chilton for several years. The surfaces of her work are always uneven and the tensions in the many materials she uses, from felt to silk to fine papers, always vary. After much experimentation I have decided that dry mounting generally offers the best form of adhesion for her felt-based artwork, as the dry mounting process heats up the felt and makes it much easier to mount flat. However, dry mounting is only allowable at Minimum and Budget Levels and is not recommended for work of any value.

I always use reversible dry mounting tissue and conservation mountboard. While this process is still not acceptable at Commended Level and above, it is possible to reverse the bond: I know, because I have done it. However, adhesive residues may remain and dry mounting does alter the original condition of the artwork. Framers must make sure that customers are aware of the implications before proceeding and must ask their customers to sign a disclaimer.

In the end, however, I chose not to dry mount the three textiles shown here. Instead, a mixture of different techniques had to be used.

The three pieces of work were inspired by the Minoan frescoes of the Palace of Knossos on Crete. They reflect both the images of the frescoes, the animals and birds which so fascinated the Minoans, and the many artifacts that have been discovered on the site. The two smaller pieces are made from lightweight fabrics, including chiffon and silk. The third and largest, of a 'necklace' of fish strung along a line, is made from the same fabrics but is also sewn onto hand-made paper and a lightweight felt. The pieces had to be handled very differently.

Linda wanted the whole of the fish artwork to be visible in the frame but had left very little felt with which to mount it. I therefore attached it to a piece of unbleached cotton and tacked all round with cotton thread, creating a secure and stable base and giving myself enough surplus with which to attach the work to the mount.

If you need to stitch a textile onto a donor fabric, this should always be weaker than the artwork itself. Any stress must be borne by the donor piece, so that, should a tear or rip occur, it is the donor fabric rather than the artwork that will be damaged.

I cut a piece of conservation mountboard slightly smaller than the total area of the cotton fabric and used tapestry tape to stretch the artwork over the board. Tapestry tape leaves an acidic residue, but in this instance it was only in contact with the cotton backing, not the artwork itself.

The next step was to design a mount to reflect the theme of the artwork. The idea with the fish piece was to allow the raw edges to extend over the edges of the mount, to create a feeling of freedom and spontaneity. The two smaller textiles would sit on top of this first mount. I decided to arrange the three fabrics in portrait fashion, with an aperture in the centre for the largest piece.

Since the textiles are several millimeters thick in some places I used a double mount to distance them from the glass. The top mount was first cut with 'dovetail corners', then 'two step long corners' were added to the second mount. These mountcutting techniques are fairly complex and are described in detail in my book The Art of Mountcutting, published by the Fine Art Trade Guild. I cut some small decorative shapes from mountboard in two colours, which I hoped echoed the style of Minoan decoration, and glued them into the corners with PVA glue.

Once these two top mounts were complete, I affixed 5mm foam board fillets between them to achieve the right spacing. I cut the foam board into 50mm strips with bevelled edges, as these are more discreet than straight-cut spacers. I cut the bevel by placing a trapezoidal or craft blade in the bevel blade holder of my mountcutter. This enabled me to extend the blade to the depth needed to cut through the foam board without producing an uneven or wobbly cut. The pieces were then fixed together.

Now to the third mount, the one on top of which two of the textiles would sit. I calculated where the centre lay and cut an aperture for the largest piece of work. I then assembled the three mounts, and set about positioning the two smaller textiles. I used small pieces of tapestry tape to hold them in place while I stitched them onto the mountboard with cotton thread.

I then put the centre textile in place, with its overlapping edges, and attached it to the back of the mount with gummed-paper tape. This tape stands the test of time better than self-adhesive tape, and it did not come into contact with the artwork itself, but with the cotton donor cloth.

The mounting job was almost done. All that was left to do was to even up the levels of the work where they differed. For example, the central textile was deeper than the windowmount to which it was attached, so mountboard fillets were added at the sides to ensure uniform depth and to keep the artwork flat.

I then cut the back board and glass. I taped all these materials together into a 'sandwich' with gummed-paper tape along all four edges, which offers some protection against the ingress of dirt, dust and insects, but still allows the various components to breathe. Finally, the sandwich was fitted into a frame made from a light ash moulding.

Making an irregularly curved frame measuring 4m long to fit a mixed-media tapestry
By Peter Cleevely GCF, Picture Corner,
www.picturecorner.co.uk

The irregular curved frame was made from pieces of 8cm flat maple veneer.

My client, a local authority, was adamant that the tapestry by weaver Julieann Worrall Hood should be in a curved frame that follows the lines of the artwork. Apparently, the curve is important as it was designed to reflect the shape of the room in which the work would eventually hang.

We decided that an 8cm flat maple veneer would flatter the artwork, without in any way overpowering it. This moulding would also complement the décor of the room, which is dominated by substantial brown wooden furniture.

I began by getting in touch with various engineering companies to ask whether a steel template could be manufactured to enable us to steam and bend the moulding into the desired shape. It quickly became clear that this would be prohibitively expensive and I was also doubtful whether it would be possible to maintain an even curve in a moulding that size.

Our only option was to cut the moulding into sections that, when joined, would follow the required curve.

The tapestry was already attached to its support. The council had fixed the tapestry to 15mm board with Velcro, which was sewn around the back edges. The board was cut to size with a jig-saw, then the rough edges had been smoothed down and the other half of the Velcro was stapled to the board. Since the piece of board was so large we had to clear out the workshop and arrange a couple of poster browsers for it to rest on, before it was delivered.

We began by drawing a scaled-down template of the back board, on which we marked corner angles, lengths and the angles of the shorter sections that would fit together to form the curves at the top and bottom of the frame. The shape was so irregular and the angles so out of square that each section would have to be shaved in order to fit together.

The top consisted of nine sections, the shortest of which measured 185mm and the longest 600mm. The angles varied between 2 and 4 degrees. We measured the corner angles with a vernier protractor borrowed from an engineering company; the top two corners were 82 degrees, the bottom right was 88 degrees and the bottom left was 90 degrees.

We cut the nine top sections slightly too large, so that they would be the right size once the angles had been cut out. The next stage was to cut the angles. The fencing on the Morsø had to be turned inwards, towards the operator, so that the moulding could be shaved and angles of 2 and 4 degrees could be cut.

Once shaved, the pieces were laid across the top of the back board and some were returned to the Morsø for further shaving, so that the angles fitted snugly together. Safety was paramount throughout as no guards or stops were in place to protect our fingers.

Once the pieces were right, they were underpinned to produce the large top curve. This was temporarily taped into position on the back board, so that the other three sides could be positioned to fit.

We tackled the two sides next. The corner angles were shaved to fit; then the sides were fitted to the back board.

We were now in our second day and were beginning to relax and enjoy the challenge. The continual flow of customers into the gallery meant that word was going round that Picture Corner was up to something unusual. We benefited from quite a bit of media attention.

The bottom curve consisted of eight pieces, varying in length from seven that were 180mm to one that was 480mm. The same process of shaving and joining was undertaken. The next stage, underpinning the four sides, needed a lot of space, so the gallery was cleared and the underpinner carried through from the workshop. Three people were required to hold and join the four sections.

A final fitting was carried out before joining, to ensure that the frame fitted the back board properly. The tapestry was attached to the back board on its

Velcro strips; the frame was carefully positioned over it and screwed to the back board with brass screws.

Once a sufficiently large van had transported the tapestry to the council chambers, it was hoisted up onto the wall and secured with brass plates.

Framing a mixed-media quilt
By Mal Reynolds GCF Adv, Harlequin Frames,
mal@harlequinframes.f9.co.uk

The mixed-media textile is in a double-sided frame, so it can be viewed from either side. It is supported on a rail and secured at the bottom corners with brass wire. Seen here is the front of the textile.

Framing mixed-media textiles is always a challenge, particularly as in this case when a double-sided frame is required, but proper preparation and attention to detail can eliminate most problems. In the framing of fabric art the same questions arise at the outset each time; in this case, the major issues were how to support the quilt and how to design the frame so that both sides could be seen. Before addressing these two issues I had to take a good look at the textile itself and assess its properties.

Yvonne Brown creates contemporary wall hangings and embroideries. She has a passion for fabric, threads, texture and colour, and constantly seeks to

Looking down into the frame at the brass eye and wire which anchors the textile and slightly tensions it.

explore ways in which she can use textiles as an artistic medium to produce images with a tactile surface that have a richness and depth not often possible by more conventional means. Yvonne finds inspiration in the natural world and from art historical sources, particularly the medieval period.

Designed and created in 2005, *Helianthus I* was inspired by the glorious fields of sunflowers of Provence, with their wonderful heads following the sun. The textile has a machine quilted background on hand-dyed cotton. The sunflower heads are layers of sheer, synthetic fabrics on a background of synthetic felt; the design is machined onto the layered fabrics and cut back with a fine-tipped soldering iron. The work is finished with hand beading and each of the small sunflowers is hand embroidered. *Helianthus I* was originally made to enter the Small Wonders category at the 2006 Chicago International Quilt Festival and was then exhibited at the Houston International Quilt Festival. It has subsequently been featured in Quilting Arts Magazine, April/May 2007.

Normally, quilts are hung vertically, from a pole, either through hoops attached to the top of the quilt or through a sleeve sewn onto the back. The artist had sewn a sleeve onto the back of this piece and when I used 20mm dowel to support the quilt it did not hang as I wanted. The sleeve bulged out round the dowel and I realised that to achieve the best fall I would need to use a rectangular wood support, which would hold the quilt flat.

I called Yvonne, who kindly sent me some of the hand-dyed cotton that forms the background of the work. I wanted to use this to cover the wooden support; this would look aesthetically pleasing and would form a barrier between the wood and the artwork. I began by sealing a 35x8mm wood support with two coats of PVA; then I covered the parts which would show, or come into contact with the artwork, with the material using aqueous EVA.

The quilt needed support at the bottom, both to prevent it flapping about in the frame and to slightly tension it, which would enhance its appearance. I sewed the 'D' part of two D-rings into small loops of material, which were lightly sewn to the back of the quilt in the bottom corners.

I used brass picture wire, rather than thread, to tension the quilt. The wire was attached to both Ds at one end and was stapled to the frame at the other. I used brass wire as it looked good aesthetically and I knew that there would be no dangers caused by over-tensioning, as the wire would slip away from the staples, or the stitches round the D-ring would come loose, before undue pressure was exerted on the fabric.

The wire was threaded through holes in the mountboard lining at the bottom of the frame, and I inserted eyelets into the holes for added strength and because these look professional, should anyone peer down behind the windowmount. Conscious that the stapled wire would cause bumps in the mountboard lining, I chiselled two small indents out of the moulding that would 'contain' the secured wire. These would of course be hidden by the mountboard lining.

The box frame was constructed from an obeche moulding with a depth of 50mm, which provides sufficient distance between the glass and the quilt, even taking into account the fact that the tips of the sunflowers are not secured to the main part of the quilt.

The box frame also formed the 'back frame'; remember that this was a double-sided frame so that the artwork could be seen from the back as well.

The back of the textile, showing the loop of fabric attached to the D-ring.

The back of the textile, showing the fabric-covered rail which supports the textile.

I used the moulding upside-down, so that the lip of the moulding was at the back, holding the glass in place.

I hung the quilt from its support in order to establish the size of frame required. I don't like artwork to look cramped; images of all kinds are flattered by space around them to breathe, so I generally allow about 10 per cent of the image size around the edges. I cut the moulding very carefully, with small bites on the Morsø, as the rebate supports did not reach the rebate (had this been a harder wood, or if numerous pieces were required, I would have made an extension to the rebate supports).

Once each section of frame was cut, I carefully measured the positions for both the support and the areas to be chiselled out for the brass wire. For the support, I cut a hole in one of the vertical pieces of moulding to a depth of 5mm. The hole at the opposite side went right through the moulding, allowing me to insert the quilt when the construction of the frame was complete.

The inside of the moulding was coated with PVA to give a stronger bond when attaching the mountboard lining. This is a handy trick I learnt many years ago; the PVA forms a skin so that when you apply more PVA or sticky tape at a later date you can achieve an extremely good grip.

The frame was then glued and pinned. I managed to stack three 15mm wedges, first using an off-cut to test that these would not pierce the edge of the frame. To provide added support, the top edge of the moulding was nailed with 20mm framers' nails, which were punched into the moulding, and then the holes were filled.

The frame was painted with a mottled effect and similar colours to those in the fabric. I applied two layers of undercoat, then a coat of green. I then mixed

projects

The supporting rail seen from the front.

a variety of browns and reds and stippled these onto the frame with a sponge, before adding dark blue to the mix and repeating the stippling process. Finally, I coated the frame with a watered-down yellow wash and wiped away the residue; I did this several times until I achieved the desired effect.

The glass and windowmount for the back of the frame were then cut to size. The aperture of this mount was 5mm smaller, on each side, than the front windowmount, to ensure that it would not be visible when viewing the finished frame from the front. Ordinary float glass was used at the back.

The brass picture framing wire was stapled into the base, the glass was cleaned and the back frame was assembled.

The mountboard used to line the box was cut to size. Cream mountboard was chosen because the tone, colours and speckled effect were reflected in the sunflowers, and because these properties lightened the inside of the box, drawing one's eyes directly to the quilt.

I inserted two eyelets into the mountboard lining. I then cut a rectangular hole at each side of the mountboard lining to accommodate the support; these were cut at 90 degrees and they followed the same outline as the holes in the frame. The mountboard lining was attached with double-sided tape in the usual way: that is, the top and bottom sides first, then the two vertical pieces second so they would offer additional support to the top and bottom pieces.

Having completed the box, I turned my attention to the front frame. I chose a moulding in colours and with a mottled effect that complemented the quilt. The frame was cut to size and the windowmount was cut.

As usual when I frame collectable textile art, I used conservation glass. Once this was cut to size, all that was left was to fix the quilt to its support, fasten it into the box and then complete the final assembly.

The cloth-covered support was inserted in the sleeve at the back of the quilt, and the textile was put into the frame. When attaching the wire to the D-rings I realised that small modifications were needed to the lower supports to ensure that I achieved the correct tension. After some experimentation, I attached the D-rings at a slight outwards angle and moved the eyelets towards the edge of the box-frame. This entailed cutting the bottom piece of mountboard again and inserting the eyelets in different positions.

Following a final check on the positioning of the quilt the front frame was attached to the box with multipoints and was taped with gummed-paper tape. The tape covered the join between the two frames and the hole where the support was inserted. Since this frame is part of my own collection, I painted the tape as I had the box-frame, and then waxed the whole thing. However, commercially I would only offer to decorate the box. Because I was prepared to be flexible and modify my ideas as work progressed, I ended up with a superbly finished piece of work which demonstrates what, I believe, can be achieved through attention to detail and 'thinking outside the box'. Like most projects of this kind, the design and planning stage were time-consuming, but

The back of the framed textile.

projects

I could complete a second frame of this type much more quickly, making it an economically viable project.

I believe there is a strong market for framed fabric art as more embroiderers look to raise the profile of their work. But are we as framers ready, and, most importantly, qualified and able to meet this demand?

Framing a Permin needlepoint
By Mal Reynolds GCF Adv, Harlequin Frames,
mal@harlequinframes.f9.co.uk

I am always on the lookout for additions to my embroidery collection so was

Many framers feel that woollen needlepoint is not flattered by paper windowmounts, whereas this hessian-covered slip complements the colours and texture of the stitched artwork.

delighted to come across a needlepoint produced by the Permin Company of Copenhagen and dated 1938. I was told that this particular needlepoint, which has a Celtic theme, may have been one of Permin's samples. The needlepoint is stitched on duo or penelope canvas in both wool and silk thread, the white stitches being silk. The threads have not faded; they are as true and vibrant as the day they were stitched, indicating that the piece had been kept away from the sun and well looked after.

The needlepoint is roughly 30cm square and features two types of stitch:

tramming and tent stitches. Tramming is a technique whereby a thin thread is stitched onto the fabric, in some cases before printing, and is commonly used on duo or penelope canvas to help define the design. The needleworker then overstitches the tramming threads to produce the finished work, which has a raised appearance. In this case, some of the tramming stitches were left visible which gives an interesting finish.

The tent, or half cross stitch, is the most common stitch used in needlepoint and can be sewn diagonally either from left to right, or from right to left, depending on whether the embroiderer is right or left handed. This will also determine the direction of the parallelogram if the needlepoint is not square.

Fortunately this needlepoint had already been squared, so I could turn my attention to the frame design. Traditionally needlepoint goes straight into a frame without a windowmount, so I decided to use a slip to ensure that the threads would be safely distanced from the glazing. My chosen slip, which would go under the glass, creates an 8mm gap between artwork and glazing, which is ample. I lined the slip with archival frame sealing tape to protect against acid leaching from the wood and damaging the canvas.

I found a moulding for the frame that had a sufficiently deep rebate to accommodate the glass, slip, supported needlepoint, undermount and back board. I thought that I might need to construct a box frame, so was pleased when I worked out that this would not be necessary.

I decided to lace the needlepoint over 2mm off-white conservation quality mountboard. I held the artwork over various shades of board, but found that this best complemented the work. When lacing, it is essential that the mountboard is cut square. The slip had a 7mm 'lip', so I had to ensure that this would conceal the minimum amount of the stitched area. The mountboard

support was finally cut to 315x325mm; then the sharp cut edges were removed with an artists' bone.

The centres both of the needlepoint and of its support were marked in pencil. These were then aligned and the work was pinned with T-pins, starting at the centres then moving outwards, with pins inserted at intervals of about 15mm. It should be easy to align the warp and weft whilst pinning, so long as the mountboard is square. I began by pinning just the two slightly longer sides that were to be laced first. (I always lace the long sides first, though in this case the artwork is almost square.)

I laced using a ballpoint tapestry needle and mercerised cotton, starting at the edge, and then sewing at a distance of 20mm to the far edge. I then experimented with the tension before tying off the thread. This process was repeated for the shorter sides; then the corners were neatly folded and sewn in place.

The slip was lined with the sealing tape, then mitred and joined ensuring that no wood was exposed at the join. I checked that the needlepoint fitted snugly in this inner frame then cut an undermount from 1650 micron mountboard. This was to protect the underside of the stretched needlepoint from any acid leaching from the MDF back board.

The frame was then mitred and joined. I used conservation quality 'invisible' glass, which would both offer some protection from damaging UV light and ensure that the needlepoint looked its best and was not distorted by annoying reflections.

Once assembled, the artwork, support, undermount, slip and glazing stood proud at the back of the frame by about 0.5mm. I therefore cut the MDF back-board to fit onto the moulding, rather than into it, and pinned it in place with framers' pins. The back was then taped with gummed-paper tape, to finish it off and protect against the ingress of dirt and insects. Finally, hangers and felt bumpers were attached.

Framing a 2m dragon, covered head to toe in sequins and semi-precious stones
By Nicholas Muschamp GCF, Ltd Space

The whole of my counter was covered with a shimmering Oriental dragon as

The 2m dragon, which is covered in sequins and semi-precious stones, was laced over 3mm jumbo mountboard.

my customer slowly unravelled the bulky fabric. The dragon is covered in sequins and semi-precious stones and is 28mm thick. I expect that the expression on my face said it all.

We discussed the piece for about half an hour. For aesthetic reasons we decided to use two frames. The inner one would lift the glazing away from the fabric, which was important because some of the padded areas were nearly 30mm thick, and the outer or top frame would hold the glazing in place.

It was no easy task to find two compatible frames; we spent a long time combing through catalogues and looking at samples. Finally, we decided upon a gold and black scoop moulding for the inner frame; this was perfect because of its high reverse which was able to lift the glazing. The outer frame

The glazing is held in place between two different mouldings.

had a deep rebate which could accommodate the inner frame, so that the whole would look like one frame.

The first job was to buy 2m of black fabric, which we cut into strips and sewed around the outer edges of the artwork, as there was not enough spare fabric to enable us to stretch it. I sewed using ordinary cotton, but with very small close stitches that would be able to stand the weight of the fabric.

I then had to decide upon the type of board over which to stretch the fabric, which was difficult given its size and weight. Luckily we had some 3mm jumbo board left over from a previous job, which we carefully cut to size allowing about 7mm all round to accommodate the rebate and stretching.

The next job was to lace the fabric over its support. I began by placing the board on my workbench and positioning the artwork on top, aligning the corners and sticking a few pins along the outside edges through the fabric and into the board, which temporarily held the artwork in place.

The artwork was then turned face-down, ready for lacing. I used strong thread that would be able to tension the work, but would not pull too tightly. I laced the long sides together first, taking care not to tension the piece too tightly. It soon became apparent that the lacing would be a long and laborious task, but that this method would give the best results due to its flexibility and reversibility.

We repeated lacing along the remaining two sides, periodically checking alignment, before finally adjusting the tension and tying the thread. Two and a half hours and 100m of thread later, I was in need of some light refreshment.

I needed to stitch around the padded areas, as the weight and volume of the piece required extra support to prevent sagging. Armed with a sharp needle, black cotton and a thimble, I set about stitching through the fabric and board around the central raised areas. I had to sew about 120 tacks, which gave me aching fingers and thumbs. After every few stitches I tied the cotton into a loop and started again.

When cutting and assembling the inner frame, I had to be sure that the fabric fitted snugly into it. The outer frame was also cut to fit snugly over the inner one. Because of the size and depth of the piece, I had to use 3mm glass.

The stretched fabric and a 2.5mm back board were securely fixed into the inner frame with framers' points. I then examined the artwork very carefully for those little gremlins that framers love. Once I was satisfied that the fabric art looked its best, I positioned the glass on top of the inner frame and 'encased' it with the outer frame.

I then turned it face down. The deep rebate and snug fit meant that final assembly was straightforward. The final job was to tape around both frames at the back.

I ended up undercharging for the job, as I underestimated the time that it would take. My advice would be to add on half as much time again as you initially thought that such a job would take. I thought that this job would take about five hours, whereas it probably took more than a day. Remember that ordering unusual materials, such as jumbo board and 3mm glass, takes time and that complicated jobs require a lot of time-consuming discussion with the customer. In this case, I also spent a lot of time searching for two frames that were compatible both visually and structurally.

glossary

Acetate Fabric derived from either cotton or woodpulp that has undergone further processing thus classifying it as synthetic. It reacts badly to strong heat and high concentrations of alkalis or acids. Acetate is an unusual base for fabric art.

Acid Acid attacks paper and fabric fibres by shortening them, causing them to discolour, become brittle and eventually turn to dust. Exposure to light and damp accelerates this process. Acid is generated by the lignin (tree sap) in paper. It is also in some of the chemicals used to make paper, adhesives and framing materials. Atmospheric pollution can also cause acid damage to artwork over time. Conservation framing materials and techniques are designed to protect artwork from attack by acids.

Acid burn Discolouration caused by acid migrating onto artwork, often from the cut edge of the windowmount.

Acid free Containing no acid. A misleading term often used to describe board, paper or adhesive that has been treated to give a pH value of more than 7. Bear in mind that however 'acid free' a material may have been rendered during manufacture, over time chemicals from processing or atmospheric pollutants may lead to the formation of acid. This imprecise term should be avoided.

Acid-free tissue paper This is pH neutral tissue paper which should be used when storing fabric art. Its composition renders it harmless to fabrics, even those stored for long periods of time. Fabrics and items of clothing can be 'stuffed' with pH neutral tissue paper to give them shape before framing.

Acrylic A modern man-made fabric that is lightweight, crease resistant and flexible. It can be produced in many different weights, some of which are suitable for use as embroidery background cloth. It cannot be dyed.

Acrylic glazing A generic term used to describe plastic alternatives to glass. Acrylic glazing is lightweight so can be useful when framing large items. It is often used on work that is to hang is public places and children's rooms for safety reasons. 'Perspex' and 'Plexiglas' are the brand-names of types of acrylic glazing.

Adhesive There are many types of adhesive or glue; some are water soluble, and thus reversible, and some are not. Glue can be used to stretch and stick fabric art to a support board; it should be spread along the edges of the back of the support and the fabric pulled onto the back. It is not acceptable to use glue when framing to Museum or Conservation Levels, though fully reversible pH neutral water-based adhesive may be used on washable fabric art at Commended Level. Non-reversible clear adhesives may be used at Budget and Minimum Levels, but are not recommended.

Aida cloth Aida cloth is a woven fabric with a specific quantity of stitches per inch. Cross stitch is usually sewn onto aida. It is available in many colours. Because you can see through aida, it is important to choose the colour of your support board carefully. If a lot of travelling threads are visible, it may be sensible to place a dark board behind the embroidery in an attempt to mask the problem, though it should be noted that this could influence the final colour of the fabric.

Alkaline The opposite to acidic. Alkaline materials are used in conservation framing and have a pH reading greater than 7. Calcium carbonate is commonly added to paper as an alkaline reserve, to counteract the paper's natural degradation, acidic inks and acid in the atmosphere. Alkaline reserves added to paper are often called 'buffers'.

Anti-reflective glazing Glazing that reduces reflection and maximises image clarity.

Appliqué The name given to a method of applying a design in one fabric onto a background of another type of fabric. Appliqué can take many forms, and may be attached by hand stitching, machine stitching or even glue. Depending on the depth of the appliqué, it may require framing as a 3D object to ensure that it is distanced from the glazing. Heavy bits of ornamentation may need individual support when framing.

Assisi work A type of embroidery where the background is sewn in cross stitch leaving the design plain. The design is sometimes emphasised with brightly coloured edging stitches. A type of traditional Italian stitchwork.

Back board The back of a picture frame. Back board was traditionally made from hardboard or plywood, which are highly acidic, but there are lightweight pH neutral alternatives available today. Back board can be made from a range of materials including foam board, MDF, chipboard and greyboard. Pulpboard and cardboard are acceptable as back boards for Minimum and Budget Level framing jobs, and it is not necessary to include a 'barrier layer' between the artwork and the back board. At Commended Level there should be a barrier layer underneath the artwork, unless a quality combination undermount / back board is used. It is essential to use undermounts of the appropriate quality at both Conservation and Museum Levels.

Barrier board Board that is placed between the undermount, or support, and the back board as a protective layer.

Bargello Sometimes known as Florentine or longstitch work, designs are worked on canvas in vertical stitches. The stitches (known as satin stitch) are offset from one another creating a wavy or zig-zag pattern. The entire canvas is normally covered with stitches.

Ballpoint needles Needles with a blunt point. They stitch into the holes on cloth (for example, canvas or aida) and do not pierce the surrounding threads.

Ballpoint pens These should never be used for any framing project, as the ink may be harmful. Marks on windowmounts, etc. should be made in pencil.

Batik Designs that are applied to cotton using wax and dye. Batiks often come from the Far East or Africa. It is important for the customer to identify the correct way round for the image since the back is very similar to the front. Signatures also need to be the correct way round. Before stretching, batik should generally be placed between two sheets of brown paper or tissue and ironed. The heat will release any excess wax, which will be absorbed by the paper. Inexpensive batiks can often be successfully dry mounted, as the cotton is flat.

Beadwork The process of adding beads to stitchwork. Spacing is essential when framing beadwork to ensure that the 3D effect is not lessened or flattened by the glazing. Beads and similar items are susceptible to water damage.

Bespoke Made to the customer's specific requirements. 'Custom' is the US term for bespoke, so they use 'custom framing' rather than bespoke framing.

Blackwork A type of embroidery where black threads are used on white or cream fabric defining geometric designs, which probably indicates an Arabic or Moorish influence. The technique often combines cutwork and drawn threads.

Bleed, bleeding Giving up colour in water or other solvent. It is essential to check that fabrics and threads are colourfast and do not bleed before steaming artwork or using water-based solvents. (Also see 'Colourfast'.)

Blocking This is the American term for squaring (see below).

Blue Wool Scale A method of quantifying the lightfastness of colours. Blue Wool Scale 6 is fade resistant.

Box frame A deep frame designed to display 3D objects. Box frame mouldings with deep rebates can be bought by the length, and framers often extend mouldings with their own 'build-ups'. Box frames are generally lined with mountboard or foam board and the interior may be painted or covered with fabric. Box frames are also referred to as 'shadow boxes'.

Broderie Anglaise A type of embroidery combining running and satin stitches with cutwork, usually small round or oval eyelets. When stretching, care needs to be taken to maintain tension throughout the cutwork and stitching.

Canvas An open-mesh material that forms the foundation for needlepoint. It is available in two basic types, single-thread (also known as mono), and double-thread (also known as penelope). Both are produced in a variety of sizes and fibres: cotton, acrylic, linen and plastic. Single-thread canvas is easier for counting stitches, but double-thread is stronger and therefore more suitable for large pieces of work. The plasticised variety does not stretch well.

Carpet tape This heavy-duty double-sided tape can be used to stretch fabric art of little value, but it will leave a residue and cannot be guaranteed to stand the test of time. Carpet tape is only acceptable at Budget and Minimum Levels.

Cellulose fibres Fibres derived from plants, not animals. The most common types are cotton and linen, but the following are also in this group: jute, ramie, sisal and hemp.

Colourfast Colourfastness is the process of testing whether dyes in threads and fabric are resistant to bleeding or running. Colours can be tested with great caution using a cotton bud and distilled water on small samples of thread, or on the back of needlework. Conservators do not recommend this method but it is commonly used.

Congress cloth A firm cloth, similar to canvas, but of very fine gauge, typically 25 threads per inch. Congress cloth is primarily used for crewel and gold work but also for very fine cross stitch and sampler-type work.

Conservation The process of preserving and protecting artwork. Conservation framing involves materials and techniques that do not alter the original condition of the artwork, and will protect it in the future. Conservation framing is called 'preservation framing' in the USA. Conservation differs from restoration (see below).

Conservation mountboard Board suitable for framing to Conservation Level, as defined by the Fine Art Trade Guild's Five Levels of Framing, but is not suitable at Museum Level. Conservation mountboard is made with chemically purified woodpulp or cotton fibre with an alpha cellulose content of no less than 84 per cent.

Cord Many framers prefer to hang pictures with nylon cord rather than wire, as it is less likely to become brittle and fail, and it is easier to work with. The main drawback of cord is that it can sag over time and require tightening. Another modern alternative is plastic coated picture wire.

Cotton Cotton comes from the seed heads of the cotton plant and the quality varies depending on its place of origin. It can withstand high temperatures and can be stored for long periods without deterioration. However, cotton can yellow with exposure to light and becomes brittle if in contact with wood. It is not generally attacked by insects (unless dirty), but silverfish do enjoy a meal of cotton, particularly if it is starched. Cotton fibres are stronger when wet than dry.

Cotton museum mountboard This board is sometimes called museum board, all-rag board or cotton board. It is made from 100 per cent cotton fibres, rather than wood fibres, including all facing and backing papers. It is free from impurities and must have a pH range of 7.5 to 9.5, including lamination adhesives. Dyes and pigments must be non-bleeding, lightfast and resistant to abrasion. Cotton fibres are not inherently acidic so do not require chemically purifying, but are buffered to protect them against acids that may be absorbed in the future. This is the only type of board that can be used when framing to Museum Level.

Couching This term describes a way in which threads can be held in place. A long thread is placed on top of the fabric and a 'couching' or looping thread is used the entire length of the long thread to hold it in place. In Oriental embroideries, gold threads are often 'couched' with orange or red silk, giving a corded appearance.

The 'count' This refers to the number of holes per inch of fabric (for example, people refer to '16 count fabric').

Counted cross stitch The stitcher works on a blank piece of fabric, transferring the design from paper onto the fabric by counting threads. Background fabric is often left as part of the design. Great precision is required since an error in the counting process alters the design.

Crewel This old fashioned form of embroidery usually depicts birds, flowers, etc. Traditionally the work was stitched onto linen, cotton or wool using a woollen thread. The design is outlined in chain stitch and is very often worked on a dark background.

Crochet This term is derived from the French word 'crochet', meaning hook. A continuous thread is wound and pulled into loops on a crochet hook. Different types of winding and looping produce different shapes and designs. The final work looks like lace but is produced with much heavier threads.

Cross stitch The formation of an embroidery stitch by crossing threads into a small 'x'. The size of the x's depends on the size of the squares in the fabric. Due to the open weave of the fabric, neat finishing off at the back is important. Kits can be purchased which include everything you need to undertake a cross stitch. Either the design is printed on the fabric or there is 'counted cross stitch' (see above). Cross stitch is often sewn onto aida cloth (see above) but experienced stitchers use a range of fabrics including linen.

Cutwork A style of stitchwork that incorporates stitching and open areas, a bit like lace. A design is worked on the fabric and, once completed, areas are snipped away to form holes (for example, a flower may be stitched and the centre may be cut out to form a hole). It is a process commonly used in the Far East and generally the work is 'white on white'. Cutwork is found in antique stitchwork.

De-ionised water This contains no ions other than hydrogen, oxygen and hydroxyl ions. It has been chemically purified.

Diffused glazing This type of glazing is etched to reduce reflection in harsh lighting conditions and it can distort the image slightly. It is sometimes called 'etched glazing' and in the USA is referred to as 'anti-glare glazing'.

Distilled water This type of water is used by conservation framers. Tap water contains impurities and chemicals, and the minerals in mineral water are of an unknown quantity. Distilled water has been boiled, vapourised and collected in controlled conditions.

Donor fabric Sometimes a piece of fabric art requires attachment to a donor fabric, either to give it strength or to enlarge the size for easy handling and stretching. Care must be taken when choosing the donor fabric because not all fabrics are pH neutral. Silk has a very high acid content and should be attached to a different cloth of a similar weight, such as lawn or very light cotton.

Double mount Two windowmounts are used to surround the artwork, the lower one projecting a few millimeters beyond the top one. This creates extra depth, thus distancing artwork further from glazing, and can be aesthetically pleasing. Framers often use a conservatively coloured top mount with a brighter lower mount that mirrors one of the colours in the artwork.

Double-sided tape This comes in various strengths and can be used to attach fabrics of no commercial or sentimental value. The adhesive will not stand the test of time and is likely to stain the artwork so it is only allowable at Budget and Minimum Levels. Double-sided tape is often used by framers when making double mounts and box-frames; in these cases, the tape is not in direct contact with the artwork, and once framing is complete the board is held in place by the structure of the frame.

Drawn fabric work See 'Open work' below.

Dressing This starch-like substance is used to stiffen fabric and canvas. After hours of embroidery, fabrics tend to soften. Washing can sometimes help to redistribute the dressing so that it becomes uniform, while needlepoint on canvas needs to be squared (see below).

D-rings Fittings that are attached to the backs of frames to which cord or wire is tied. Many framers prefer D-rings to screw eyes as they allow the frame to hang closer to the wall. D-rings can be attached to the back board for small pictures, or to the moulding for heavier ones.

Dry cleaning The process of cleaning by solvent, not water. A professional dry cleaning establishment can carry out spot cleaning but the process is not suitable for antique fabrics.

Dry mounting Dry mounting involves sticking down artwork with 'dry' solvents that do not involve the addition of water. Dry mounting can be carried out with spray-on adhesives, self-adhesive boards or tissues that are heat or pressure activated in a press or roller. Dry mounting is an acceptable way to flatten and bond low value unstitched fabrics that do not contain wool or 3D embellishments. Reversible dry mounting tissue is available, though reversion can be extremely difficult and time-consuming. Dry mounting is not suitable for old, valuable or damaged embroideries and fabric art. The pressure required to form a bond would detrimentally squash the stitches in sewn work, so dry mounting is best suited to fabrics such as batiks. Any uneven surfaces will become more noticeable once fabric is dry mounted. These methods are only allowed at Budget and Minimum Levels.

Embroidery A generic term describing the decoration of fabric by needle and thread. There are hundreds of different stitches and types of embroidery, and any type of fabric can be embroidered.

Embroidery hoop A frame designed to hold fabric whilst it is embroidered. Hoops are round, but rectangular frames are also available. The fabric is tightly tensioned, which makes it easier to hold and stitch evenly. If an embroidery has taken a long time to complete or has not been carefully stored, frame marks may be left on the fabric once it is removed. It is recommended that the hoop be removed at the end of each embroidering session and replaced when you are next stitching.

Even weave Fabric with an even weave can be used for counted cross stitch, as it is easy to count the threads and sew a consistent design. Even weave fabrics with a count of between 22 and 28 are often used for counted cross stitch.

Fabric Fabric is made from threads, which in turn are made from fibres.

Fabric art A generic term incorporating all art made mainly from fabrics and threads.

Fillet A small 'frame' made from narrow decorative strips of wood, which protrudes from under the windowmount. Fillets distance artwork from the glazing and can be aesthetically pleasing.

Fabric extensions Some fabric art has insufficient borders for stretching, so strips of fabric are sewn around each side.

Fibres Threads consist of fibres, which can be manufactured from man-made or natural products. Man-made fibres include metallic threads, rayon, nylon, polyester, synthetic velvet and acrylic; these are more susceptible to heat damage than natural fibres. Natural fibres can be harvested from animal or vegetable sources; silk and wool are animal-based, whilst cotton and linen are made from vegetable fibres. (Also see 'Cellulose fibres'.)

Fine Art Trade Guild The trade association representing the interests of all art and framing professionals, *www.fineart.co.uk*

Fishing line This transparent 'thread' comes in various strengths and can support considerable weight. It can damage delicate fabric. Fishing line is not intended for long-term use, so it yellows and becomes brittle over time and is not recommended.

Five Levels of Framing Standards for framing established by the Fine Art Trade Guild to help framers explain their work to customers. The levels help customers compare framing jobs and can be useful in the event of litigation. There is a description of the Five Levels on p135.

Float glass Ordinary picture framing glass, which is normally 2mm thick.

Float mounting The process whereby artwork is framed with all four edges showing. It is normally adhered to board with a reverse cut bevel, which is in turn secured to an undermount, so the artwork appears to 'float'.

Foam board A composite board with a foam centre and papered back and front, available in standard and pH neutral qualities. It is extremely light, rigid and versatile and can be used to stretch small lightweight fabric in conjunction with T-pins. Foam board is used to make box frames and thick covered mounts and as back board. It is sometimes referred to as 'foam core'.

Foxing Unsightly brown spots that can appear on the front of artwork, particularly art on paper. These are caused by fungus growth and acid stains in the framing materials or the artwork itself. Removing foxing marks is a job for a professional conservator.

French matting The US term for windowmounts decorated with washes, lines and gold colouring.

Glass size See 'Rebate size'.

Glazing Describes both glass and plastic alternatives to glass.

Glue See 'Adhesive'.

Gross point This term refers to the size of stitches and canvas. Gross point has less than 16 holes per inch. (Also see 'Needlepoint'.)

Gummed-paper tape Water-activated tape which forms a bond that can be reversed by the addition of water. This type of tape should be used for conservation framing (hinges made from Japanese paper and hand-made starch paste are an alternative). Gummed-paper tape should create a bond that lasts for longer than one achieved with pressure-sensitive tape. The water-soluble adhesive does not leave an acidic residue. Gummed-linen tape is preferred by some conservation framers.

Hardanger Small and delicate Scandinavian stitchwork. It is worked on 22 count fabric, so there are 22 threads per inch. The fabric is woven with paired vertical and horizontal threads and whilst the cloth looks similar to aida cloth, the weave is much less visible. The stitch work is the same as cross stitch though smaller.

Hinging When conservation framing works on paper, the artwork is generally attached to the undermount with T-shaped hinges attached to the back of the artwork. Some small, rigid, lightweight pieces of fabric art can be supported using this technique up to Commended Level.

Holes in fabric Fabrics with holes or damaged weaves should be handled with extreme care. To mask a hole, either place a piece of similarly coloured material on the support board or paint the board under the hole to make it less noticeable. Use water-resistant paints (for example, acrylic).

Humidity The percentage of water retained in the atmosphere. Very low humidity can cause hygroscopic materials to cockle and flake, while high humidity can cause mould and accelerate the process whereby materials become acidic. A constant relative humidity of around 55 to 60 per cent is best for storing hygroscopic works.

Image size The measurements of artwork that are to be visible within the frame and windowmount, including borders, if these are to show. Image size is not always obvious and can be a matter of taste (for example, a customer may want a tiny image surrounded by a large expanse of paper or fabric). Image size is sometimes referred to as 'window size', since it is the size to which the window aperture is to be cut.

Iron-on vylene Sheet fabric impregnated with adhesive that is activated by heat from an iron. It comes in varying weights and can be used to attach fabric to fabric. This product is sometimes used at Budget and Minimum Levels as a way of stiffening small embroideries instead of stretching them, but note that the shape cannot be adjusted if the fabric is out of square.

Knots Embroideries with knots at the back are extremely difficult to lay flat. Ideally, loose ends should be sewn in so there are no knots, as these will show at the front. If squaring a needlepoint with lots of woolly knots at the back over a piece of board, square it face inwards so that the process does not exaggerate the bumps at the front. Knots can sometimes be disguised by padding (see below).

Lacing This is the traditional method of stretching fabrics that are sufficiently strong. It is usual to stretch over mountboard or foam board of the appropriate quality. The thread used for lacing should be of the same weight as the fabric or slightly lighter; if there is a problem, the lacing threads should break, not the fabric. The thread should be a continuous length that is pulled through with each stitch from side to side and then from top to bottom at even distances apart. Tension is achieved by pulling the continuous thread. This method is time-consuming and therefore an expensive method of stretching. Lacing is appropriate when framing to Museum Level, though sometimes at this level it may be appropriate to use a donor fabric (see above).

Lightfastness The likelihood of dyes, pigments and paints changing hue when exposed to daylight, heat, acids or alkalis. Lightfastness can be measured by laboratory tests such as the Blue Wool Scale (see p120). Exposure to UV light accelerates fading. (Also see 'Colourfast').

Lignin The substance that binds the cellulose fibres in wood and paper. Lignin turns to acid, which causes paper made from wood to discolour and weaken. It is chemically unstable and highly light and heat sensitive; lignin becomes acidic as it breaks down.

Linen Linen is a natural fibre obtained from the flax plant. The fibres carry water up the stem and are very absorbent. Its quality varies depending on growing conditions, age, etc. It has a high cellulose content, but is not as pure as cotton. Linen becomes dark and brittle when placed against wood. It is stronger when wet, washes well and can be dry cleaned. Counted cross stitch is sometimes sewn onto linen with an even weave and a count of between 25 and 35.

Long and short stitch A type of embroidery that entirely covers the canvas and is similar to needlepoint. The stitches are vertical and can vary in length from very short to very long. Tensioning the fabric can be difficult because of the different stitch lengths, and great care must be taken to avoid distortion of the threads. Over-tensioning by the stitcher can cause problems.

Marks on fabric Marks can be introduced in a number of ways. Hands give off natural grease, which eventually yellows the fabric, and this grease in turn can attract dirt. Use of embroidery frames can leave marks, so it is best to remove them at the end of each stitching session. Marks which are not too obvious unframed will 'leap out' once behind glass. Valuable fabrics should be handed over to a conservator for cleaning. See the sections on 'Washing' and 'Stains and stain removers', Chapter 1: Before framing, p17.

Masking tape Cheap self-adhesive tape designed for temporary use. Not only is it acidic and therefore harmful, but it will leave a residue that can be impossible to remove. Masking tape is likely to fail more quickly than other tapes and is not suitable at any framing level.

Mat, matting, matboard US terms for mountboard (see below).

Mercerised cotton Cotton that has been chemically treated to increase its strength, lustre and resistance to mildew, as well as to reduce lint. Mercerised cotton is useful for lacing fabric art.

Metallic threadwork This thread is manufactured from gold leaf, silk and paper and requires careful handling. Originally real metals were incorporated into embroideries, but metallic threads are now more commonly used. They are often held in place with couching threads and great care must be taken when stretching to avoid distorting them. Care must also be taken to avoid getting them damp or wet because of discolouration and corrosion.

Mixed-media work A work that combines two or more methods of production, such as a textile embroidered in a range of stitches and types of thread with additional 3D embellishments.

Morsø A mitre guillotine for cutting picture frame mouldings. Morsø is the brand name of a machine made in Denmark, which is the market leader, so has become the term commonly used to describe any frame mitring machine.

Mouldings Lengths of wood, aluminium or plastic designed to be mitre-cut to form picture frames. Mouldings can be decorated with a range of paint finishes, embossed, laminated, veneered or gilded. A huge array of designs is available, in varying widths, depths and price brackets. Some mouldings are sold unfinished so that framers can apply their own finishes by hand.

Mountboard Board specially made for creating windowmounts (see below). Mountboard comes in three qualities: cotton museum, conservation and standard. See the Fine Art Trade Guild's Mountboard Standards at *www.fineart.co.uk/Mountboardstandards.aspx*. The Guild's Five Levels of Framing explain which board is suitable for each type of framing.

Mountcutters Mountcutting machines are used by framers to cut windowmounts. Manual versions replaced the traditional method involving a scalpel blade and a metal ruler a few decades ago, and now computerised mountcutters (CMCs) are becoming widely used.

Museum mountboard See 'Cotton museum mountboard'.

Natural fibres Fibres that occur in nature. Animal or protein fibres include wool and silk, while vegetable fibres include cotton and linen.

Needle art Another term for embroidery, describing the decoration of fabric by needle and thread. There are hundreds of different stitches and types of needle art, and any type of fabric can be embroidered.

Needlepoint This term describes any embroidery on canvas where the whole of the canvas is covered by stitching. The term includes gross point, quick point and petit point. Needlepoint often needs squaring before stretching. The term 'tapestry' is often used to describe needlepoint, which is inaccurate as tapestries are actually woven, rather than sewn.

Needles Different types of embroidery require different needles. Needlepoint is always worked with a blunt (ballpoint) needle so that it passes through the weave without damaging the material. Crewel needles are more commonly used for fine embroidery since they are short, have a long, slender eye and are very fine at the sharp end so pass through fabric easily. They are numbered 1-12 to denote size: the higher the number, the finer the needle. Like pins, needles come in many different sizes. Normal sharp needles can pierce threads and are available from extremely fine to very thick. Too thick a needle on silk will leave an unsightly hole. (Also see 'Ballpoint' and 'Tapestry' needles.)

Newberry method A method of stretching fabric over foam board with T-pins, and then fitting the stretched work back inside a foam board 'frame'. This method is suitable at Conservation Level if pH neutral foam board is used.

Normal conditions The term as used in the Guild's standards means out of direct sunlight, within a temperature range of 10 to 25 degrees centigrade and relative humidity between 40 and 60 per cent.

Nylon Man-made fibre first introduced in the 1930s. Nylon washes well, but can go yellow if subjected to high temperatures. It is not affected by bleaches, and should only be ironed on a very low setting to avoid melting and softening. Sometimes used as a flexible base for 3D fabric art.

Open work As the name suggests, this type of embroidery has an open effect. Holes are produced by pulling threads together to reveal open designs. The stitching is worked on loosely woven fabric where the threads can be easily counted. A ballpoint or blunt needle should be used to avoid penetration of the fine threads. Open work is also referred to as drawn-fabric work and pulled-thread work.

Oriental embroidery Oriental embroidery is usually stitched onto silk, which comes in a vast range of weights and textures. It often incorporates stitching and couching with metallic threads (see above). High quality embroideries are usually set with Japanese rice paste on the rear and can take many months or years to complete. Silk threads are always used; these are spun and twisted to the correct size as required. Oriental embroideries should never be washed and only a conservator should undertake cleaning. Sometimes Oriental embroideries are finished off with a sewn-on border. These borders can cause problems when stretching because it is difficult to regulate the tension when two fabrics have been joined; the mixing of different fabrics often causes puckering.

Overcut When cutting an aperture in a windowmount, the framer may inadvertently extend the cut a millimetre or two beyond the corner, so a small cut line is visible, which is considered unprofessional.

Padding Polyester padding can be used to pad fabrics. This helps to disguise knots and uneven tensions in fabric art and is particularly effective behind silk embroideries, which are difficult to stretch without rippling. Padding provides a luxurious 3D appearance, although this is minimised when behind glass. Foam padding is not suitable because it degrades and dis-colours with age. Self-adhesive board with padding attached is available.

Papyrus Papyrus is not a fabric; it is woven from wet reeds taken from a papyrus plant. Tourist souvenirs from Egypt are commonly painted onto papyrus.

Petit point This type of needlepoint is sewn on fine canvas and delicate designs can be produced. Petit point is usually sewn at between 16 and 40 stitches to the inch on single-thread canvas. (Also see 'Needlepoint'.)

pH scale A scale for measuring the acidity and alkalinity of materials. The range is 0 to 14; a reading of pH7 is neutral, while more than 7 is alkaline and less than 7 is acidic.

Pins Pins are used in various methods of stretching fabric art and different sizes should be used according to the type of fabric you are stretching. Inferior quality pins can rust and corrode causing irreparable damage, while stainless steel pins do not corrode. Nickel plated pins are acceptable at Budget and Minimum Levels, and stainless steel ones should be used at Conservation and Commended Levels. It is not acceptable to use pins when stretching fabric art at Museum Level.

Polyester Man-made fabric that is extremely hardy. Polyester is easy to wash but can go shiny if pressed with too hot an iron. It can be used as a back-ground cloth for needlework.

Pressing Pressing improves the appearance of many types of embroidery, as it removes creases and adds life to flattened stitches and pile. Care must be taken when pressing as many types of fabric art are damaged by heat and the moisture in steam.

Pressure-sensitive tape See 'Self-adhesive tape'.

Profile The shape or cross-section of a picture frame moulding.

Puckered Different tensions within a sewn fabric can lead to puckering. This may occur if part of a fabric is heavily embroidered, with an expanse of unsewn fabric; puckering means that the fabric art will not lie flat, even if it is squared. Puckering can be disguised with padding.

Pulled-thread work See 'Open work'.

Quick point Needlepoint on large-mesh canvas of five to seven holes per inch, which is sewn with thick yarns. (Also see 'Needlepoint'.)

Rayon Rayon is a synthetic silk fabric and can be produced in many different textures and weights. It creases very easily unless it has been made crease resistant. Viscose is a type of rayon, and is the least expensive to produce.

Rebate The depth of a picture frame moulding. Mouldings with a deep rebate can be used to make box frames. It is called the 'rabbet' in the USA.

Rebate size The outside measurement of the artwork, windowmount and undermount, i.e., the size which the moulding must be cut to accommodate. Also referred to as the glass size.

Re-generated fibres Natural fibres that have been dissolved and then extruded as filaments that can be spun together, such as rayon.

Restoration Returning damaged artwork to a state similar to its original condition. Restoration implies a greater level of intervention than conservation (see above); conservation is the process by which artwork is preserved rather than repaired. Restoration should be carried out by qualified experts, as amateur attempts can do more harm than good.

Reversible Reversible materials and techniques can be undone, so the artwork is returned to its original condition. At Museum, Conservation and Commended Levels, framing must be easily reversible.

Samplers Originally this term referred to embroidered 'test pieces'. Antique samplers are highly collectible and the value depends very much on the condition. In the past, all young ladies were taught to sew and embroider and a lot of samplers incorporate many practice designs and stitch types arranged in a decorative form. They usually incorporate text, such as the worker's name and age or the alphabet. They require careful handling and should be framed to at least Conservation Level.

Self-adhesive mountboard Board with a sticky surface can be suitable for stretching flat fabrics such as silk and cotton at Budget and Minimum Levels. The bond may not be reliable if the fabric is textured or stitched. The use of self-adhesive mountboard is a method of dry mounting (see above).

Self-adhesive tape This type of tape tends to leave an acidic residue when removed, though water-soluble pH neutral self-adhesive tapes are being introduced. It also lasts less long than tape which has to be damped. The use of self-adhesive tape is not acceptable when conservation framing.

Selvage Differently finished edging or border on cloths and fabrics.

Shadow boxes See 'Box frames'.

Sight size See 'Image size'.

Silicone sealer This is sold in DIY shops for sealing around baths, etc. Silicone sealer is used by framers when making box frames (for example, to secure glazing, attach 3D objects and make boxes).

Silk Silk is a continuous strand of protein made from the cocoons of silkworms. Light and hot, dry conditions make silk dry and brittle. It can yellow when exposed to sun, and will lose some of its breaking strength if in continuous sunlight. Silk is weaker when wet and therefore dry cleaning is a safer option. When damaged, silk is impossible to repair. Silk thread is very strong.

Size A dilute mixture of gluey or resinous substance which is applied to some threads and needlepoint canvas to stiffen and protect them during sewing, as well as to reduce absorbancy. Size makes the materials more durable and easy to handle. Once this is washed away after sewing, needle art can look fresh and reinvigorated. Some size includes acidic components, so washing it away before framing also helps preserve the artwork. Paper is also treated with size during manufacture, so that inks do not bleed and the paper is smooth.

Smocking Fabric is gathered into measured folds and by stitching across the folds, attractive and decorative designs are created giving elasticity to the fabric. Care needs to be taken when stretching to avoid distortion of the original design.

Spacers Strips of wood, plastic or board that are hidden under the lip of the moulding and are used to distance the glazing from the artwork. Spacers can be used instead of, or as well as, a windowmount. They are sometimes covered with fabric or painted.

Squaring Squaring describes the manner in which hand-sewn needlepoint is pulled into shape; the stitcher inevitably pulls the fabric out of square when sewing. Squaring normally involves water or steam to make the fibres more pliable. Squaring is called 'blocking' in the USA, and 'steam blocking' is a US term for squaring by steam.

Standard mountboard All mountboard which does not meet the Fine Art Trade Guild's specifications for cotton museum and conservation mount-board must meet the requirements for standard board as a minimum. Otherwise, it should not be used for professional framing. See *www.fineart.co.uk/Mountboardstandards.aspx* for the standards in full.

Staples Stapling can be used to support fabric art of little value, from small cross stitches to heavyweight woollen needlepoint. They can also be used when squaring needlepoint. Staples split threads and are very unyielding so are only suitable for Budget and Minimum Level framing.

Steam blocking See 'Squaring'.

Stretcher bars Some framers stretch heavy needlepoint over stretcher bars, using either diagonally placed staples or copper pins. Depending on the level of framing, the bars can be covered with a tightly wound fabric (such as cotton) or covered with mountboard. A sheet of fabric or board can also be fitted behind the fabric for added protection and to prevent staining from airflow and dust. Stretcher bars are suitable at Commended, Budget and Minimum Levels.

Stretching The process of tensioning fabric art over a support, prior to placing it in its frame. Fabric expands and contracts so without stretching it would eventually lose its shape. Most fabric needs to be stretched prior to framing, whereas only hand-sewn needlepoint on canvas needs squaring.

Support The framework or board over which fabric art is stretched. Fabric may be attached to its support in many ways including lacing, pinning and dry mounting.

Support cloth See 'Donor fabric'.

Synthetic fibres These do not occur naturally but are manufactured. Synthetic fibres, such as nylon and polyester, react badly to heat and may even melt. Viscose is less vulnerable to heat.

Tag guns Hand-held guns that shoot tags between 4mm and 6mm to attach fabric to mountboard and foam board. Tag guns are commonly used when framing clothing such as sports shirts. The use of tag guns is acceptable up to Commended Level, and at Conservation Level for items of a coarse or open weave, if care is taken not to break threads.

Tapestry Commonly used term for needlepoint (see above), which is the correct term for hand-sewn designs of this type. Genuine tapestry is actually woven, not stitched.

Tapestry needle The thickest type of needle available. They have a large eye, since most tapestries are sewn in wool. They are available in a variety of sizes and are similar to chenille needles. Tapestry needles are blunt so that they do not pierce the threads or cloth.

Tapestry tape The tackiness of this product falls somewhere between normal double-sided tape and carpet tape. It can be used to stretch fabric art of little value but all tapes of this nature leave a residue and cannot be guaranteed to stand the test of time. Tapestry tape is only acceptable at Budget and Minimum Levels.

Tension The level of tightness in a stitch. Embroideries can be made up of thousands of stitches and it is important that each one is consistent if uniform tension is to be achieved. If the tension is good, the stitching will be flat and the fabric should stretch satisfactorily. However, if the tension is uneven, the fabric can pucker and, no matter what you do, you will never get it to square or flatten properly. Most problems occur on fabric that is partially embroidered; the tensions are very different and the blank pieces of fabric will not lie flat. To hide uneven tension, it is sometimes beneficial to pad the work.

Tent stitch Standard needlepoint is sewn with the same under-and-over stitch throughout, which is called tent stitch.

Textile A generic term describing fabric or material.

Thread Fine cord of spun-out fibres of flax, cotton, silk, wool, etc. Fabrics are made from threads. Two or more threads twisted together make sewing threads. Embroidery silk is the common name given to the large variety of threads available for all types of stitchwork.

Tie-dye The process of dying fabric where the fabric is bunched either by knotting or by tying with string or elastic bands. When the fabric is immersed in dye, the tied areas are left uncoloured, thus forming large circular designs.

T-pins T-shaped stainless steel pins. They are extremely useful in conjunction with foam board or thick mountboard; the pin is pushed into the edges to secure the fabric and stretching is easy because the pins can be moved until the work is perfect. At Conservation Level fine quality stainless steel pins of the thinnest gauge should be used, which are known as silk pins.

Travelling stitches If you hold a piece of work up to the light, you can see where threads have 'travelled' from one part on the back of the work to another. Once the work is laid down on a base, these threads will show more clearly, though an undermount of the appropriate colour can help minimise the effect.

Triple mount Three windowmounts are used to surround the artwork. See 'Double mount' for an explanation.

Tufted wool embroidery This type of embroidery incorporates dense loops of all sizes; the stitcher cuts the loops when the work is complete to give a 3D-pile effect. Used for rugs and cushions.

Tweezers An invaluable piece of equipment. Stray hairs or threads which fingers are too big to remove can be lifted with tweezers.

Ultra-violet (UV) light The invisible light at the violet end of the spectrum that causes paper and some fabrics to deteriorate and discolour, as well as fading some colour pigments. UV light is a major threat to the longevity of many types of artwork. Specialist UV-filtering glazing (see below) can help protect artwork though it is still best not to hang vulnerable work in direct sunlight.

Undermount This is the surface onto which artwork on paper is normally attached and is generally made from mountboard 1100 microns thick or more. The undermount forms a protective layer between the artwork and the back board. When framing fabric art the artwork is stretched over a support, and barrier board (see above) is sometimes positioned between the support and the back board.

Underpinner The machine used by framers to insert 'wedges' into the bottom of mitre-cut mouldings to form picture frames. The wedges join the four sides together and should be used in conjunction with adhesive to form a secure bond. DIY framers tend to use clamps and pins to join frames; this method is slower and the pin holes at the sides need filling.

UV-filtering glazing Glazing incorporating a layer that filters out a percentage of damaging UV light. This is more expensive than standard 2mm float glass, but is used by conservation framers.

Velcro Fabric incorporating two compatible strips, one covered with tiny hooks, the other with loops. When pressed together Velcro can provide a strong and tight bond.

Velvet Velvet is a soft piled fabric used for backgrounds and covering the insides of boxes. It can be manufactured from a variety of man-made or natural products and has a short, dense pile. The denser the pile, the better the quality. It should not be ironed, but can be steamed. Cleaning should only be carried out by an expert.

Warp and weft These names refer to the construction of fabric, which is produced from interlocking fibres at right angles to each other. The warp runs from top to bottom and the weft runs from side to side. Imagine an old weaving loom: the warp threads are attached to the front and back of the machine, while the weft produces the selvage edges (weft = west-east).

Water soluble Substances that dissolve in water, as opposed to oil. Water-soluble substances are used in conservation framing as they are reversible without the use of solvents.

Wedges Small triangles of wood that are inserted into the corners and cross-over points on timber stretcher bars. These can be gently 'tapped in' with a hammer if the artwork shows signs of sagging. Stretcher bars are some-times used when squaring needlepoint, and tapping in the wedges can help adjust the tension. The term 'wedges' is also used to describe the little metal right angles that framing underpinners shoot out to join two pieces of mitred moulding.

Wet mount To stick down artwork with 'wet' paste and water. Wet mounting can be done with water-soluble paste, but is still not acceptable to conser-vators as the back of the artwork is coated with paste, which alters its original condition. Many framers find dry mounting (see above) to be a quicker and less messy method of framing non-valuable artwork.

White core This denotes the colour of the core of some mountboard, and its ability to remain white over time, and does not imply that conservation standards have been met.

White work This term covers all types of embroidery where white threads are used on white fabric. It often combines cutwork and drawn threads to create different effects.

Windowmount Mountboard with an aperture in the middle, used to surround artwork and distance it from the glazing. Double and triple mounts can be aesthetically pleasing and further increase the distance between artwork and glazing. Windowmounts can be decorated with paints, powders and papers and mountboard comes in a wide range of colours and textures. Care should be taken to use the appropriate quality mountboard for each framing task; the Five Levels of Framing explain this. (Also see 'Mountboard'.)

Wool Wool becomes dry, hard and brittle if deprived of moisture. It can decompose when left in direct sunlight and reacts unfavourably to heat. Wool fibres shrink and mat together if washed and rubbed in hot soapy water. Wool can easily scorch so if it has to be ironed; work on the wrong side with the iron on a low setting and preferably iron through a cloth.

Wool work This term refers to any embroidery worked in wool.

Yarn Strands of fibre (cotton, wool, silk or flax) that are spun together and used in weaving and knitting.

appendix one
five levels of framing

The Fine Art Trade Guild, the trade association representing the interests of art and framing professionals, has identified Five Levels of Framing. These provide a consistent benchmark of standards that enable people to make informed choices when choosing framing, and allow them to compare quotations on a 'like-for-like' basis. People can see, for example, why one framer might quote more for a job than another. The levels also assist the Guild when arbitrating in disputes revolving round whether a given specification has been met.

Below is a summary of the specifications. Please note that these are regularly updated to take into account current best practise. They can be seen in full on the Guild's website at *www.fineart.co.uk/framingstandards.aspx*.

Museum Level (highest specification)
Objective
The objective is to visually enhance the artwork and offer the ultimate level of protection from physical and mechanical damage, airborne pollution and acids from framing materials for up to 35 years in normal conditions. It is recommended that a 'condition of artwork' report is made prior to framing and that appropriate remedial action is advised before re-framing. Ideally, the framer or conservator should examine the frame every five years and there should be a label advising this on the back of the frame.

Suitable for
Museum quality works and artwork that is to be preserved for the future, including high value items and artwork of potential or historical value. Processes must be fully reversible. Customers should be advised that lifetimes given assume that artwork is not inherently unstable.

Moulding
There should be no significant blemishes. Care must be taken to match the pieces. The moulding should have a rebate that is sufficiently deep to comfortably hold the sandwich. If artwork is likely to touch the moulding, this should be sealed with strips of cotton museum mountboard or a conservation foil and paper tape. Note: good original frames should be retained wherever possible as these can enhance the value of the artwork. Mitres must be accurately cut, glued and pinned tightly. Corners to be touched-up so no unfinished moulding is visible.

Windowmount
A windowmount or slip should normally be used to visually enhance the

artwork and distance it from the glazing. If close framing is required, there should be a spacer between the artwork and the glazing and this should be made from cotton museum mountboard. The corners of the windowmount must be cleanly cut; the mountboard must be free from blemishes and there must be clearance of 1-3mm inside the rebate (clearance varies depending upon frame size). Only cotton museum mountboard at least 1100 microns thick and conforming to Guild standards should be used. Slip moulding must be accurately cut and should not touch the artwork. Multiple mounts or deep spacers must be used to frame works with migrant or delicate pigments, such as pastel drawings or artwork with cockled surfaces. Using a fixative on pigments is not acceptable. The windowmount should, where possible, project at least 5mm over the edge of the artwork, thus holding it firmly in place. Any pencil marks on the underside of the windowmount should be rubbed out as they may come into contact with the artwork. For photographs, unbuffered cotton museum mountboard should be used. Note: sometimes it is advantageous to retain an original windowmount (possibly gilded or decorated). In this case, preferably 1100 micron, but at least 500 micron, cotton museum quality mountboard barrier should be cut to fit the underside of the windowmount to within a few millimetres of the aperture or a few millimetres beyond the opening.

Undermount

There should be a barrier layer between the artwork and the back board; this should be made from cotton museum board of an appropriate thickness, at least 1100 microns thick. For photographs, unbuffered cotton museum mountboard should be used. The undermount should be the same size as the windowmount and hinged to it along the longer side using museum quality paper or fabric with either starch paste or SCMC (sodium carboxyl methylcellulose). Note: artwork stuck down onto acidic board should be referred to a conservator for possible removal of the board.

Attaching artwork

The artwork should be hinged to the undermount with T-hinges, along the top edge, or a similarly reversible process should be used, such as corner pockets made from naturally lignin-free museum quality paper. It is not acceptable to makes hinges from self-adhesive tape; hinges should be made from naturally lignin-free, pH neutral paper and adhesive from starch paste or SCMC. Hinges should be torn, not cut. Hinges should be weaker than, or the same paper weight, as the artwork, never heavier. Hinges should be attached to the back of the artwork, not the front, and should overlap onto the artwork by the minimum amount necessary to give proper support. Note: for the majority of art on paper, 5mm should be sufficient. Artwork should be hinged to the undermount, not to the back of the windowmount. Artwork must be properly centred and free from blemishes caused by framing.

Glazing

Glazing must be free from obvious blemishes and of appropriate thickness for the frame size. Preferably museum quality glazing should be used, i.e., glazing that blocks more than 90 per cent of all UV rays (unless the picture is going to hang where there are already controlled UV levels, such as some museums). The glazing must be cut to allow sufficient clearance inside the rebate of the frame. It is not acceptable for the glazing to touch the artwork. For large items and for items to be hung in areas accessible to the public, safety should be considered (for example, laminated or acrylic sheet may be advisable). Final cleaning fluid should contain only de-ionised water and perhaps industrial methylated spirit.

Back board

Needs to be strong, rigid and flat (for example, hardboard or MDF with a 500 micron barrier board, or Melinex board or similar, in addition to the under-mount, pH neutral back board or foam board). It must be cut to allow sufficient clearance inside the rebate.

Securing the frame

It is recommended that glazing, mounts and artwork are sealed together with gummed conservation quality paper tape with water-soluble adhesive, before being fitted into the frame to keep out dust, insects, etc. The frame must be secured with framers' points, tacks or better; flexible tabs are not acceptable.

Hanging

Hanging fittings must be sufficiently strong to support the frame. Riveted D-rings are only acceptable for lightweight works if the customer has chosen a thin moulding, in which case an additional undermount should be used.

Finish

Dust and dirt should be removed and the glass should be cleaned and polished without smears. It is not acceptable to seal the back with self-adhesive tape; gummed-paper tape must be used and this must be carefully applied. Pads or buffers should be applied to the two lower inside corners. A label giving the date and the framer's name should be adhered to the back. Note: any existing labels should be preserved as they can provide provenance for the artwork.

Notes on framing fabric, canvas and objects at Museum Level

Fabric should be squared if necessary. It is not acceptable for fabric to be stuck-down or stapled or to use any process which may damage the fabric. It should either be hand-sewn onto a backing cloth with the appropriate thread, or be laced over a museum quality support, or similarly reversible methods should be used. Unsightly problems, such as knots or travelling stitches, must be concealed where possible. If fabric touches the stretcher bars, these must be sealed.

Canvas must not sag/bow or tear/distort. Stretchers must be square and sufficiently strong to stand the test of time. Corner wedges must be held in place with thread. The rebate must be around 3 to 6mm larger than the stretcher bars.

Objects must not be held in place with adhesive or silicon sealer. Loops of thread must be used, or objects must be held in place between museum quality boards or with special chemically inert supports.

Conservation Level (second highest specification)
Objective
The objective is to visually enhance artwork and offer a high level of protection from physical and mechanical damage, airborne pollution and acids generated by framing materials, for approximately 20 years under normal conditions. Consumers should be advised that frames should be examined every five years and this advice should be added onto a back-of-frame label.

Suitable for
Collectable artwork that is to be kept for future generations, such as original paintings and limited edition prints of moderate to high value, as well as items of sentimental value. Processes must be reversible. Customers should be advised that lifetimes given assume that artwork is not inherently unstable.

Moulding
There should be no significant blemishes. Care must be taken to match the pieces. The moulding should have a rebate that is sufficiently deep to comfortably hold the sandwich. If artwork is likely to touch the moulding, this should be sealed with strips of thick pH neutral fabric, conservation mountboard or a conservation foil and paper tape. Good original frames should be retained wherever possible as these can enhance the value of the artwork.

Windowmount
A windowmount or slip should normally be used to visually enhance the artwork and distance it from the glazing. Pencil marks should be rubbed out where in contact with the artwork. If close framing is required, there should be a spacer between the artwork and the glazing and this should be made from conservation or cotton musuem mountboard or plastic. The corners of the windowmount must be cleanly cut; the mountboard must be free from blemishes; there must be clearance of 1-3mm inside the rebate (clearance varies depending upon mount size). Conservation or cotton museum mountboard at least 1100 microns thick and conforming to Guild standards should be used. Slip moulding must be accurately cut and should not touch the artwork. Multiple mounts or deep spacers must be used to frame works with

migrant or delicate pigments, such as pastel drawings, or artwork with a cockled surface. The windowmount should, where possible, project at least 5mm over the edge of the artwork, thus holding it firmly in place. For photographs, unbuffered mountboard should be used (this is only available in cotton museum quality). Note: sometimes it is advantageous to retain an original windowmount (possibly gilded or decorated). In this case, preferably 1100 micron, but at least 500 micron, conservation or cotton museum quality mountboard barrier should be cut to fit the underside of the windowmount to within a few millimetres of the aperture or a few millimetres beyond the opening.

Undermount
There should be a barrier layer between the artwork and the back board; this should be made from conservation or cotton museum quality mountboard at least 1100 microns thick. For photographs unbuffered mountboard should be used. The undermount should be the same size as the windowmount and hinged to it with a gummed conservation tape and water-soluble adhesive. Note: artwork stuck down onto acid board should be referred to a conservator for possible removal or the board.

Attaching artwork
The artwork should be hinged to the undermount with T-hinges, along the top edge, or a similarly reversible process should be used, such as corner pockets made from conservation or museum quality materials. It is not acceptable to make hinges from self-adhesive tape; hinges should be made from conservation or museum quality tape and water-soluble adhesive. Hinges should be attached to the back of the artwork, not the front, and should overlap onto the artwork the minimum amount necessary to give proper support. Note: for the majority of art on paper 5mm should be sufficient. Artwork should be hinged to the undermount, not the back of the windowmount. Artwork must be properly centred and free from blemishes caused by framing.

Glazing
Float glass or better, free from obvious blemishes should be used. Glass with high UV protection should be considered. It must be cut to allow sufficient clearance inside the rebate of the frame. It is not acceptable for the glazing to touch the artwork. For large items and for items to be hung in areas accessible to the public, safety should be considered (for example, laminated or acrylic sheet may be advisable). Final cleaning fluid should contain only de-ionised water and perhaps industrial methylated spirit.

Back board
This needs to be strong, rigid and flat, and to protect the artwork from damage. It must be cut to allow sufficient clearance inside the rebate.

Securing the frame

The frame must be secured with framers' points or tacks; flexible tabs are not acceptable.

Hanging

Hanging fittings must be sufficiently strong to support the frame. Riveted D-rings are only acceptable for lightweight works if the customer has chosen a thin moulding, in which case an additional 500 micron barrier should be used.

Finish

Dust and dirt should be removed and the glass should be cleaned and polished without smears. It is not acceptable to seal the back with self-adhesive tape; gummed-paper tape must be used and this must be carefully applied. Pads or buffers should be applied to the lower inside corners. A label giving the date and the framer's name should be adhered to the back. Note: any existing labels should be preserved as they can provide provenance for the artwork.

Notes on framing fabric, canvas and objects at Conservation Level

Fabric should be squared if necessary. It is not acceptable for fabric to be stuck-down or stapled or to use any other process which may damage the fabric. It should be laced over a conservation quality support or similarly reversible methods should be used. Unsightly problems, such as knots or travelling stitches, must be concealed where possible. If fabric touches the stretcher bars, these must be sealed. The use of nylon tag guns is acceptable for items of a coarse or open weave fabric, but care must be taken not to break threads.

Canvas must not sag/bow or tear/distort. Stretchers must be square and sufficiently strong to stand the test of time. Corner wedges must be used and held in place with thread. The rebate must be around 3 to 6mm larger than the stretcher bars.

Objects must not be held in place with adhesive or silicon sealer. Loops of thread must be used, or objects must be held in place between conservation quality boards.

Commended Level (middle of the five specifications)

Objective

The objective is to visually enhance artwork and offer a moderate level of protection from airborne pollution and handling for around five years in normal conditions.

Suitable for

Replaceable artwork of limited commercial and/or moderate sentimental value and where visual appearance is important. Preferably, processes should be fully reversible. Customers should be advised that lifetimes given assume that artwork is not inherently unstable.

Moulding

The moulding must have no significant blemishes. Care must be taken to match the pieces. The moulding should have a rebate that is sufficiently deep to comfortably hold the sandwich. Mitres must be accurately cut, pinned tightly and glued. Corners to be touched-up so no unfinished moulding is visible.

Windowmount

A windowmount or slip should normally be used to visually enhance the artwork and distance it from the glazing. If close framing is required, there should be a spacer between the artwork and the glazing. The corners of the windowmount must be cleanly cut; the mountboard must be free from blemishes; standard quality mountboard is acceptable; there must be clearance of between 1mm and 3mm (clearance varies according to frame size) inside the rebate. Standard mountboard (or better) of at least 1100 microns should be used. Slip moulding must be accurately cut and joined. Multiple mounts or deep spacers must be used to frame works with migrant pigments, such as pastel drawings, or artwork with a cockled surface.

Undermount

There should be a barrier layer between the artwork and the back board; preferably it should be made from standard mountboard (or better) at least 1100 microns thick, but at this level 500 micron thickness may be used for lightweight artwork. The undermount should be the same size as the undermount and ideally should be hinged to it along the longer edge. Other methods of joining the two are acceptable providing no adhesive comes into contact with the artwork. Combination undermount / back boards are suitable at this level, provided each element meets the specifications.

Attaching artwork

The artwork should be hinged to the undermount with T-hinges, along the top edge, preferably using gummed paper with a water-soluble adhesive, though self-adhesive water-reversible white tape may be used, or a similar reversible process such as corner pockets. It is not acceptable to make hinges from tape with a high acid content. Hinges should be weaker than, or the same paper weight as, the artwork – never heavier. Hinges should be attached to the back of the artwork, not the front, and should overlap onto the artwork by the minimum amount necessary to give proper support. Note: for the majority of art on paper, 5mm should be sufficient. At this level, dry mounting is acceptable, providing customers understand that the process is irreversible. Artwork must be properly centred and free from blemishes caused by framing.

Glazing

Float glass or better, free from obvious blemishes and of appropriate thickness for the frame size should be used. It must be cut to allow sufficient clearance inside the rebate of the frame. It is not acceptable for the glazing to touch the artwork. For large pieces and for items to be hung in areas accessible to the public, safety should be considered (for example, laminated or acrylic sheet may be advisable).

Back board

This needs to be strong, rigid and flat, and to protect the artwork from damage. It must be cut to allow sufficient clearance inside the rebate. Combination undermount / back boards are suitable at this level, provided each element meets the specifications.

Securing the frame

The frame must be secured with framers' points or tacks. Flexible tabs are not acceptable.

Hanging

Hanging fittings must be sufficiently strong to support the frame. D-rings riveted into the back board should only be used on lightweight items.

Finish

Dust and dirt should be removed and the glass should be cleaned and polished without smears. The back should be sealed, preferably with gummed tape. At this level good quality self-adhesive framing tape may be used, but it is important to ensure good adhesion and longevity. Masking tape, cellotape and parcel tapes are not acceptable. Note: self-adhesive tapes dry out and can fail. Pads or buffers should be applied to the two lower corners. A label giving the date and the framer's name should be adhered to the back. Old labels should be retained if possible and attached to the back.

Notes on framing fabric, canvas and objects at Commended Level

Fabric should be squared if necessary. It is not acceptable for fabric to be stapled or to use any other process that may damage the fabric. It should be laced or similarly reversible methods should be used. Washable fabric art may be stuck at the edges with a water-reversible adhesive. Dry mounting may be used on fabric but is not considered satisfactory for stitching that does not lie completely flat at the back. Some attempt should be made to conceal unsightly problems, such as knots or travelling stitches. Use of nylon tag guns is acceptable.

Canvas must not sag/bow or tear/distort. Stretchers must be square and sufficiently strong to stand the test of time. Corner wedges must be used. The rebate should be around 3 to 6mm larger than the stretcher bars.

Objects must not be held in place with adhesive, though it is acceptable for small blobs of silicon sealer to come into contact with non-absorbent objects.

Budget Level (second lowest of the five specifications)
Objective
The objective is to provide a visually acceptable frame at a budget price. No pretence is made to protect the artwork or its longterm visual appearance.

Suitable for
Replaceable artwork of no commercial or sentimental value.

Moulding
There should be no significant blemishes. Mitres must be accurately cut, pinned tightly and glued. Corners should to be touched-up so no unfinished moulding is visible.

Windowmount
A windowmount or slip may be used to visually enhance the artwork. The corners of the windowmount must be cleanly cut; the mountboard must be free from blemishes; standard quality mountboard is acceptable; there must be clearance of 1mm inside the rebate. Slip moulding must be accurately cut and joined.

Undermount
A barrier layer between the artwork and the back board is not necessary.

Attaching artwork
It is acceptable for artwork to be 'slotted' into the frame without fixing or to be stuck-down. Artwork must be properly centred and free from blemishes caused by framing.

Glazing
Float glass or better, free from obvious blemishes, should be used. It must be cut to allow sufficient clearance inside the rebate of the frame. It is acceptable for the glazing to touch the artwork.

Back board
Pulpboard and cardboard are acceptable.

Securing the frame
Flexible tabs are acceptable but framers' points or tacks are preferred.

Hanging
Hanging fittings must be sufficiently strong to support the frame.

Finish
Dust and dirt should be removed and the glass should be cleaned and polished without smears. It is acceptable to seal the back with self-adhesive tape.

Notes on framing fabric, canvas and objects at Budget Level
Fabric should be squared if necessary. It is acceptable for fabric to be stuck-down or stapled. Some attempt should be made to conceal unsightly problems, such as knots or travelling stitches.
   Canvas must not sag/bow or tear/distort. Stretchers must be square.
   Objects can be held in place with adhesive.

Minimum Level (lowest of the five specifications)
Objective
The objective is to provide a basic frame at minimum cost; price overrides visual appearance and quality. (It should be noted that many of the frames available on the market fall well below the standard of the Guild's Minimum Level.)

Suitable for
Temporary display. This is an inexpensive 'cash and carry' product into which customers can insert their own artwork.

Moulding
There should be no significant blemishes. Mitres must be accurately cut, pinned tightly and glued.

Windowmount
It is not necessary to use a windowmount, but if one is used the corners must be cleanly cut and the mountboard must be free from blemishes.

Undermount
A barrier layer between the artwork and the back board is not necessary.

Attaching artwork
It is acceptable for artwork to be 'slotted' into the frame without fixing or to be stuck-down. Artwork must be properly centred and free from blemishes caused by framing.

Glazing
Rolled glass or better, free from obvious blemishes, should be used. It must be cut to give sufficient clearance inside the rebate of the frame. It is acceptable for the glazing to touch the artwork.

Back board
Pulpboard and cardboard are acceptable.

Securing the frame
Flexible tabs or better should be used.

Hanging
Hanging fittings must be sufficiently strong to support the frame. Cord and screw-eyes can be supplied for the customer to attach.

Finish
Dust and dirt should be removed. It is not necessary to seal the back with tape.

Notes on framing fabric, canvas and objects at Minimum Level
Fabric should be squared if necessary. It is acceptable for fabric to be stuck-down or stapled at this level.
   Canvas must not sag/bow or tear/distort. Stretchers must be square.
   Objects can be held in place with adhesive.

appendix two
Advanced Accreditation, Textile Framing

What is the Guild Commended Framer qualification?
The Guild Commended Framer (GCF) qualification, which was launched in 1994, is run by the Fine Art Trade Guild, the trade association for all those in the framing and art industry. Hundreds of framers have now passed the exam, which has become recognised and respected all over the world.

   Framers qualify primarily so they can demonstrate to their customers that they are committed professionals, which can give them the edge over their competitors. Even highly experienced framers claim to have found taking the exam and preparing for it to be extremely educational and thought-provoking. The Guild Commended Framer Study Guide, available from the Guild, explains what framers need to know in order to qualify and gives details of how the exam works.

   The GCF is the qualification for the general all-round framer. It has been described as testing 'excellence across the basics'. It became apparent that there was a need to recognise framers who have developed their skills to higher and more specialist levels. Thus, after a further four years' preparation, GCF Advanced Accreditation was born.

What exactly is Advanced Accreditation?

The Advanced Accreditation programme is a series of modular tests of different framing skills. Each module is a stand-alone, specific award. A framer must attain GCF status before applying for Advanced Accreditation.

Advanced Accreditation in Textile Framing was the first module to be launched. Modules in Mount Design and Function and Conservation Framing have followed. The GCF logo is enhanced with a purple ribbon for display by those who are successful in the Textile Framing module (the colour of this ribbon is different for each module).

Acknowledgements

The Advanced Accreditation in Textile Framing is the result of four years hard work, on a voluntary basis, by the Guild's Framers Committee. Their names are: Pete Bingham GCF; Trevor Davies GCF; Mary Evans GCF Adv; Lyn Hall GCF Adv; Peter Hayton GCF; Terry Jackman GCF Adv; Barry Leveton GCF; Roy Rowlands GCF; and Dave Woolass GCF. In addition, the Committee gratefully acknowledges the help and interest of Vivian Kistler CPF GCF Adv.

The scope and format of Advanced Accreditation exams

Candidates are expected to show proficiency in the following areas:
• A thorough knowledge of their subject
• The ability to assess artwork being presented for framing
• Proficiency in the techniques applicable at the different framing levels
• The ability to assess the risks involved in a job
• An understanding of the limitations of the framer's role
• The ability to handle and store artwork correctly
• Commitment to customer education
• An understanding of the relationship between the framer and conservator

Candidates are expected to use a variety of sources to acquire skill and knowledge. A thorough understanding of the contents of this book is strongly recommended.

Framers who are unfamiliar with the Guild's Five Levels of Framing are unlikely to qualify (see Appendix 1: Five Levels of Framing).

Exam format

The exam comprises three sections: inspection of framed work; practical exam; written paper.

1. Inspection of framed work

Three frames are made beforehand by the candidate. The framed pieces should have a minimum image size of 125x175mm; mounts and frames are extra to these measurements. A period of 30 minutes is allotted for this section, and the marks are 35 per cent of the total: made up of 25 per cent inspection and 10 per cent technical knowledge demonstrated during the event.

Notes on the inspection:
- The three frames to take for inspection are:
    - (a) A needlepoint, close-framed (i.e., without a windowmount) and framed to Conservation Level
    - (b) A cross stitch, or other stitched work, framed to Commended Level
    - (c) A piece of 3D fabric art to be mounted and framed to Conservation Level.
- There should be a space of 20mm or more between the underside of the artwork and the inner side of the glazing.
- Each piece should demonstrate a different stretching technique, such as lacing, pinning and gluing.
- The frames should be ready to hang but should not have identifying labels.
- Each frame should include a brief list telling the examiner what products have been used, especially where this choice relates to framing levels. This should be fixed to the back of the work.
- Candidates are required to sign a declaration that they and they alone have produced the frames. A false declaration will automatically invalidate the exam results.
- The inspection pieces may be dismantled. At the examiner's discretion they may be retained for Committee inspection, but they remain the property of the candidate throughout. Every possible effort will be made to ensure that the frames can be re-closed with the minimum of effort for later display. It is advised that artwork used should be easily portable and of low value (though it will be treated as valuable artwork).
- The inspection pieces are regarded by the Committee as an opportunity for candidates to show the true level of their ability, in both design and procedure. They should not be regarded as basic, or even average, examples.

2. Practical exam

The examiner will request a series of tasks to be performed. At least three tasks must be completed within the time allotted, which is one hour. Marks for this section are 30 per cent of the total.

Notes on the practical exam:
- Candidates are welcome to spend half an hour before the exam acquainting themselves with the site and equipment.
- Minor adjustments or recalibration of equipment are permitted.
- During the exam a candidate may decide at any point to repeat a set task. Any repeats should still be completed within the time allotted. The candidate should not ask for the examiner's advice.
- The examiner is looking for evidence of knowledge, understanding and competence. He or she may ask questions, which is not interfering or wasting time but is part of the examining process.
- The Framers Committee consider the average time for a professional framer (at GCF level) to make a 20x25mm frame to be around 30 minutes

for bespoke work in a familiar setting. This would allow for cutting and pinning the frame, glazing, a double mount and backing (up to but not including cleaning and finishing). Thus the hour allotted for three or more individual tasks is generous, and takes unfamiliar surroundings into account.

- Candidates may take their own equipment to the exam (for example, needles, threads and scissors).

3. Written paper

This comprises three parts. It lasts for 90 minutes and accounts for 35 per cent of the total marks for the whole test.

(a) A short multiple-choice questionnaire (ten questions). 10 per cent of the marks are allocated for part A

(b) A series of 12 questions which require a sentence or two to answer, and may ask for reasons or causes; 12 per cent of the marks are allocated for part B

(c) Three questions which each require up to a page to answer, from which the candidate will choose two; 13 per cent of the marks are allocated for part C.

Notes on the written test:

- Candidates are allowed time to read the instructions before starting (remember, mis-reading exam papers is the single most common error in exams).
- Answers may be in sentences, or in clear note form. The marker will not deduct marks for spelling or grammar. Clear diagrams can be included if the candidate wishes.
- A warning will be given 15 minutes before time elapses. Candidates will be asked to seal their papers into envelopes, as the examiner does not see or mark these.
- Candidates may contact the Programme Manager if they have a genuine problem over the written paper at the time of booking. Arrangements for typed answers, or taped and/or translated answers, are in place, but usually incur an extra cost such as paying an official translator.

Test centres

Exams take place at test centres, normally framing wholesalers' premises, but they can be held at candidates' own places of work by special arrangement and if a sufficient number of candidates make this financially viable.

Upon booking candidates will be provided with details about the test site and the equipment provided. They may bring any products or equipment they feel will help, with the obvious exceptions of textbooks and notes. Candidates may bring a calculator, but it must be a basic model without printer, storage or programming, and anything brought will be inspected by the examiner.

Directions and information about local accommodation will be sent with the booking confirmation.

Examiners

Examiners are appointed by the Framers Committee, which is made up of experienced respected framers. The Committee, or a member of the Guild staff appointed by them, assesses results and exam papers. Assessment is done anonymously and according to pre-set objective criteria. The examiner is not given candidates' business details.

Written tests may be arranged singly or in groups, but practical examining is on a one-to-one basis. Occasionally, a second examiner may be present; this will signify training or course moderating in operation, and has no bearing on any individual candidate.

Candidates must not be examined by someone who has trained them in textile framing. Examiners who fail to inform the Guild of such involvement are liable for de-selection, while candidates may find their exam cancelled at the last minute, without refund, if an examiner realises he or she cannot officiate. Candidates are therefore expected to inform the Programme Manager of any examiner on the current list (available from the Programme Manager), who has provided them with training.

Results and cases of partial failure

- Results will be notified by the Programme Manager, in writing, normally within two to four weeks of the test.
- A candidate may be allowed to re-take one or two sections rather than all, at the discretion of the Committee. Fees will be set accordingly in such cases.

Bookings and cancellations

- Bookings should be arranged via the GCF Programme Manager at the Guild. No queries or applications should be sent to individual examiners or test centres. Application forms and current fees can be downloaded from the Guild website, or can be posted or faxed by the Programme Manager.
- Candidates who find they cannot attend a booked test should notify the Guild at once. Fees will be transferred to an alternative date providing notification is given more than 14 days before the date booked. After that period, fees will be forfeit except in exceptional circumstances, which will be at the discretion of the Framers Committee.
- Candidates who find it impossible to attend at the last minute are requested to inform the test centre, in order to avoid unwarranted upheaval for other candidates. Please note that this is the only situation in which candidates are required to contact the test centre about their exam.

Areas of proficiency required

1. Knowledge of the main fabric types, threads, and commonly chosen base cloths: for example, the ability to distinguish between aida, linen and canvas.

2. Knowledge of the main types of fabric art and their properties: for example, the ability to identify crewel, needlepoint and batik.

3. Recognition of variables such as mixed media work: for example, the fact that parts of a piece may move in the frame (ribbons, fringes) and need to be treated separately.

4. Proficiency in a range of techniques for stretching fabric art over its support and squaring needlepoint. An understanding of the pros and cons of different methods and their adherence to the Guild's framing levels is important: for example, some work does not need squaring (un-stitched work), while light silks should be stretched over their support in a different way from heavy needlepoint.

5. An ability to assess work presented for framing. This includes the ability to examine an item, to know what to look for and why, particularly to identify problems inherent in the work.

6. Assessment of risk factors. This includes identifying fragility or deterioration and knowing how to work with this.

7. Ability to carry out the appropriate treatment, using the appropriate materials, to a high standard: for example, to square, stretch and frame a needlepoint to the desired level.

8. Handling and storing fabric art: for example, how to handle and store different weights of fabric and garments, particularly fragile items.

9. Criteria governing framing and design options.

10. Advice to clients on good practice, such as advice on handling, storing and displaying fabric art and how to protect it from light and damp.

11. The relationship between framer and conservator. The framer should have a clear understanding of their roles, and where the conservator should take over.

appendix three
useful contacts

The Crafts Council
44a Pentonville Road,
London N1 9BY
020 7806 2500
www.craftscouncil.org.uk
The national development agency
for contemporary crafts in the UK.
The publisher of Crafts magazine.

The Embroiderers' Guild
Apartment 41, Hampton Court
Palace, East Molesey, Surrey
KT8 9AU
020 8943 1229
www.embroiderersguild.com
The Embroiderers' Guild has over
25,000 members and subscribers,
238 Branches and 95 Young
Embroiderers Groups. It stocks an
extensive range of books and organ-
ises events. Publishes Stitch and
Embroidery magazines.

Fine Art Trade Guild
16-18 Empress Place
London SW6 1TT
020 7381 6616
www.fineart.co.uk
The trade association for everyone
in the art and framing industry.
Publishes *Art Business Today* magazine which includes regular articles
on framing fabric art.

Institute of Conservation (ICON)
3rd floor, Downstream Building
1 London Bridge,
London SE1 9BG
020 7785 3807
www.icon.org.uk
Includes the Conservation Register,
which can help you locate a trained
conservator in a particular field
within a geographical location.

Royal School of Needlework
Apartment 12a,
Hampton Court Palace,
East Molesey, Surrey
KT8 9AU
020 3166 6932
www.royal-needlework.co.uk
College dedicated to keeping the art
of hand embroidery alive, known for
their needlework commissions of
national importance.

Textile Conservation Centre
Winchester School of Art,
Park Avenue, Winchester
SO23 8DL
023 8059 7100
*www.textileconservationcentre.
soton.ac.uk*
A leading international organisation
in the field of textile conservation
research, education and practice.

appendix four
useful further reading

The Articles of Business
By Vivian Kistler CPF GCF
Published by Columba Publishing
Company, USA
www.columbapublishing.com
ISBN 0-938655-28-0
£17.95 from the Fine Art Trade Guild

The Art of Framing
By Piers and Caroline Feetham
Published by Ryland, Peters
& Small
www.rylandpeters.com
ISBN 9781-900518-29-5
£25 from The Fine Art Trade Guild

The Art of Mountcutting
By Lyn Hall GCF
Published by the
Fine Art Trade Guild
www.fineart.co.uk
£12.50

Conservation Framing
Published by the Fine Art
Trade Guild
www.fineart.co.uk
ISBN 0-9526294-6-1
£9.50

The Directory
Published by the Fine Art
Trade Guild
www.fineart.co.uk
An annual publication
£45

Framing Collectibles
By Vivian Kistler CPF GCF
Published by Columba
Publishing Company
www.columbapublishing.com
ISBN 9780-9386-55-29-9
£16.95 from the Fine Art Trade Guild

Guild Commended
Framer Study Guide
By Annabelle Ruston
& Fiona Ryan GCF
Published by the Fine Art
Trade Guild
www.fineart.co.uk
£12.50

Practical Gilding
By Peter and Ann MacTaggart
Published by Archetype Publications
www.archetype.co.uk
ISBN 9781-873132-83-2
£10.50 from the Fine Art Trade Guild

appendix five
framing training

A-Frame Plus
Carmashee, Kilrush Road, Kilkee,
County Clare, IRELAND
[353] 65 905 6653

Applegarth Framing
78 High Street, Repton, Derbyshire
DE65 6GF
01283 703403

Art of Framing Training School
The Workshop, Great Down, Hog's
Back, Farnham, Surrey GU10 1HD
01483 810555
www.fringearts.co.uk

Atkin Framers
Unit 101, Eucal Business Centre
Craigshill Road, Livingston
West Lothian EH54 7DT
01506 491497
www.atkin-framers.co.uk

The Bespoke Framing Company
140 Vaughan Road
Harrow
Middlesex HA1 4EB
020 8423 3535
www.bespokeframingcompany.com

Colliers
Milburn House, Dean Street,
Newcastle-upon-Tyne,
Tyne and Wear NE1 1LF
0191 232 3785/2819
www.colliersgallery.co.uk

Cregal Art Limited
Monivea Road, Galway City,
County Galway, IRELAND
[353] 9175 1864
www.cregalart.com

DIY Framing
Woodlands Farm, Burnham Road,
Beaconsfield
Buckinghamshire HP9 2SF
01494 670411
www.diyframing.com

Down School of Picture Framing
6 Church Street, Dromore,
County Down BT25 1AA
028 9269 3807
www.downschoolofpictureframing.co.uk

Galerie Lafrance
15 Pinewood Avenue, Northbourne,
Bournemouth, Dorset BH10 6BT
01202 582957
www.galerielafrance.com

Harlequin Frames
Ryland Cottage
51 Eastfield Lane, Welton
Lincolnshire LN2 3ND
01673 860249
www.mal@harlequinframes.f9.co.uk

Hedgehog Art and Framing
21 Forest Close, Lickey End,
Bromsgrove, Worcestershire
B60 1JU
01527 876293
www.hedgehog-art.co.uk

LION Picture Framing Supplies Ltd
148 Garrison Street, Heartlands,
Birmingham, West Midlands B9 4BN
0121 773 1230
www.lionpic.co.uk

Manse Studio
The Old Manse, Brecon Road,
Bwlch, Powys LD3 7HJ
01874 730115
www.christinascurr.co.uk

Northern Framing School
37 Bedford Street, Sheffield,
South Yorkshire S6 3BT
0114 272 2948

Royall Framing
Woodside Court, Hortham Lane,
Almondsbury, Bristol BS32 4JH
01454 617022
www.royallframing.co.uk

Sports Framing Ltd
24 Booth House, Featherstall Road,
Oldham, Lancashire OL9 7TQ
0161 665 2891
www.sportsframing.co.uk

Stowford Framing
Stowford Manor Farm, Wingfield,
Trowbridge, Wiltshire BA14 9LH
01225 781274
www.stowfordframing.co.uk

Village Framing
16 High Street,
Herefield, Uxbridge,
Middlesex UB9 6BU
01895 824394
www.villageframing.com

Wessex Pictures (Croydon Branch)
Unit 2b Beddington Lane Ind Estate,
117 Beddington Lane, Croydon,
Surrey CR0 4TD
020 8683 0055
www.wessexpictures.com

index

Inspired to Stitch
Stitch
21 TEXTILE ARTISTS
DIANA SPRINGALL
FOREWORD BY EDWARD LUCIE-SMITH

Inspired to Stitch by Diana Springall
ISBN: 978-0-7136-6986-2

"The anecdotes and excerpts from conversations with the artists are delightful, and the biographies and pieces themselves are inspirational."
www.fibrearts.com (Jan/Feb 2006)

"This will become a classic, justifiably so."
Textile Fibre Forum (2006 no. 81)

Other A&C Black Titles

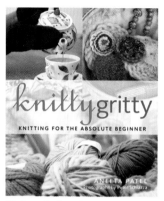

Knitty Gritty by Aneeta Patel
978-0-7136-8542-8

Paper Textiles by Christina Leitner
978-0-7136-7444-6

Nuno Felt by Liz Clay
978-0-7136-8601-2

Silk Paper for Textile Artists by Sarah Lawrence
978-1-408-10268-8

Collapse Weave by Anne Field
978-1-408-10628-0

www.acblack.com

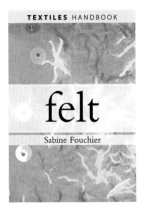

TH: Felt by Sabine Fouchier
978-0-7136-8494-0

TH: Latch-hooking Rugs
by Lynda Spiro
978-0-7136-8543-5

TH: Yarn by Penny Walsh
978-0-7136-6955-8

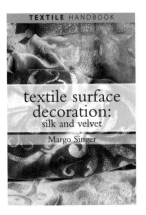

TH: Textile Surface Decoration
by Margo Singer
978-0-7136-6953-4

TH: Natural Dyes by Linda Rudkin
978-0-7136-7955-7

TH: Creative Machine Embroidery
by Linda Miller
978-1-408-10398-2